CATHEDRALS

CATHEDRALS

ROBIN S. OGGINS

MetroBooks

MetroBooks

An Imprint of Friedman/Fairfax Publishers

© 1996 by Michael Friedman Publishing Group, Inc.

Library of Congress Cataloging-in-Publication data available upon request.

ISBN 1-56799-346-X

Editor: Benjamin Boyington
Art Director: Lynne Yeamans
Designer: Stephanie Bart-Horvath
Photography Editor: Samantha Larrance
Production Associate: Camille Lee

Color separations by HK Scanner Arts Int'l Ltd.
Printed in Hong Kong by Midas Printing Ltd.

For bulk purchases and special sales, please contact:
Friedman/Fairfax Publishers
Attention: Sales Department
15 West 26th Street
New York, NY 10010
212/685-6610 FAX 212/685-1307

Visit the Friedman/Fairfax website:
http://www.webcom.com/friedman

DEDICATION

This book is dedicated to our parents: Cy and Nerma Oggins
and Chester and Ruth Darrow.

ACKNOWLEDGMENTS

My thanks to all those who told me they enjoyed *Castles and Fortresses*, in particular my former student Rosa Campa Hearne and my colleague Warren W. Wagar, and so encouraged me to undertake this work. Thanks also to Gail Kaliss, who caught a number of errors; to Jean Oggins, who read the entire manuscript and offered some excellent suggestions; and to my wife, Virginia, as always critic, editor, collaborator, and friend.

CONTENTS

OPPOSITE: View of nave at Winchester Cathedral, Hampshire, England, looking east. Winchester's nave was remodeled during the second half of the fourteenth century. The Norman pillars were cut back and refaced and the round arches were replaced with Gothic pointed ones.

CHAPTER ONE

THE ORIGIN AND DEVELOPMENT OF CATHEDRALS

The word "cathedral" comes from the Latin *cathedra*, which means "chair." A cathedral was, and is, a bishop's church—the place where the bishop has his chair.

During the earliest years of Christianity, the Church had neither bishops nor cathedrals. The Church of Jerusalem had a form of organization, but as Christianity spread, new churches in other places were not initially organized on a standard pattern. By the late first century, however, the office of bishop had developed, and by the second century the bishop (the word is derived from *episcopus*, or overseer) was the head of the local Church everywhere. By this time Christianity had become largely an urban religion, and its organization came to be patterned on that of the Roman Empire. The jurisdiction of a Roman city extended to the countryside around it—what we would call a city-state. Similarly, the bishop of a local church had authority not only over the Church in his city but also over Christians in the surrounding areas. At first, when there were few Christians, each city had only one church. But as the number of Christians grew, new churches began to be established. These new churches were headed not by new bishops, but by assistants to the bishops, and the bishop became not only the priest of his own congregation but overseer of the priests of other congregations as well.

9

During most of the first three centuries of its existence, Christianity was outlawed, and its adherents were often persecuted. Christians could not worship publicly, and it became the practice for Christians to meet in the homes of worshipers. With the growth of the Church during the second century, Christian congregations began to own property and to modify private houses for religious use. By the second half of the third century, some of these buildings were quite substantial. But not until Christianity was legalized in 313 by the Edict of Milan did truly large-scale public building by Christians become possible.

With a substantial increase in Church membership during the third century came a growing separation of both powers and functions between the clergy and the congregation, as well as a greater distinction between Christian converts and those still under instruction (catechumens). These separations were maintained physically in what has been called the hall church, in which the clergy were often seated in

PAGES 8–9: Sixteenth-century depiction of a transverse section of the basilica of Old St. Peter's, Rome. Originally built by order of the emperor Constantine, this basilica was replaced by the present St. Peter's in the sixteenth century. The term "basilica," which used to refer to an architectural type, today is a title applied to Roman Catholic churches that have been given special liturgical privileges.

ABOVE: The Roman basilica at Trier, Germany, was built by the emperor Constantine early in the fourth century. It is almost 220 feet (67.1m) long, 90 feet (27.4m) high, and 98 feet (29.8m) wide, and is one of the largest Roman buildings to have survived intact. The basilica now serves as a Protestant church.

second was constructed on the Vatican hill over St. Peter's grave. Later on, relics of saints were moved to churches and were often enclosed in a chamber below the altar. In some cases, cathedrals were built in the shape of a cross, with transepts at right angles to the nave. In general, most cathedrals built during this period were rectangular and their roofs, which were often made of wood, were flat or low-pitched like those of the Roman halls on which they were modeled.

From the fourth century on, two long-term trends had important effects on Christianity. The first was the Church's growth in power and in membership. Constantine (and his co-emperor Licinius) had legalized Christianity in 313, but Constantine went one step farther—he favored the Church and became a convert. From his reign on, all but one of the Roman emperors were Christian. The emperors gave the Christian bishops new powers and authority. In 380 Christianity became the official religion of the Roman Empire, and in 392 paganism was proscribed. In the course of some eighty years, pagan-

their own section (the chancel) at the end of the building opposite the entrance. This arrangement was similar to that of the Roman hall of justice (the basilica), in which the judge sat on a raised platform at the curved far end of the hall (the apse) in front of an effigy of the emperor. In like fashion, the bishop's chair was placed against the apse with a bench on either side for the lower clergy, while a Christian religious image (often that of Christ as ruler of the world, or Pantocrator) replaced the pagan imperial portrait. The chancel was sometimes raised higher than the body of the church (the nave) and at times separated from it by a screen. The congregation of professed Christians occupied the long nave, which was generally divided lengthwise by columns into a number of aisles, while the catechumens assembled in the vestibule (the narthex) or in the open courtyard (the atrium) outside the entrance.

Under the emperor Constantine, a number of large shrines were built over the tombs of notable martyrs, and two major basilicas were built at Rome: one was next to the Lateran Palace and became the Cathedral; a

ism and Christianity had switched places. At the beginning of the fourth century, perhaps 15 percent of the inhabitants of the Roman Empire were Christians; by the end of the century, virtually all were.

The second trend affecting the Church was a growing separation between the eastern and western parts of the Empire. Toward the end of the third century, the emperor Diocletian divided imperial authority between an eastern and a western emperor. Constantine reunited the Empire, but he moved his capital to the wealthier East, to his newly built city of Constantinople. The Empire was redivided at his death in 337 and was reunited for the last time under Theodosius, who died in 395. After that the Empire was again divided between eastern and western emperors. During the fifth century, barbarian tribes entered the Empire and conquered most of the West; in 476 the last western Roman emperor was deposed. The Balkans were invaded by Slavic peoples—a development which further separated East and West. The rise of Islam during the seventh century led to the conquest of much of the Middle East, North Africa, and

ABOVE: An interior view of the apse of San Apollinare in Classe, Ravenna, built between 534 and 549. Note the mosaic bust of Christ at the center of the triumphal arch. Here, the figure of the Cross in Heaven is the main focus of the apse mosaic.

Spain. The area surrounding the Mediterranean that had previously constituted a unified Roman Empire came to be divided into the three worlds of the Middle Ages—the Latin-speaking West, the Greek-speaking Byzantine East, and the Arabic-speaking Islamic South.

During the fifth century, a growing number of churches with domed roofs were built in the eastern part of the Empire. In the fourth century, domes had been erected over the graves of martyrs and over baptisteries; by the sixth century, domed cathedrals were being built. The most famous of these was Hagia Sophia in Constantinople, built by order of the emperor Justinian and completed in 537. These new Byzantine churches were generally square, not rectangular, with a large central dome and an interior decorated with mosaics and colored marbles. One striking feature about almost

ABOVE: Exterior of Hagia Sophia in Constantinople (now Istanbul), Turkey. The emperor Justinian's Church of Divine Wisdom, completed in 537, has been justly called "the masterpiece of Byzantine architecture." The minarets were added after the fall of Constantinople to the Turks in 1453, when Hagia Sophia became a mosque.

RIGHT: Interior of Hagia Sophia. A partial view of the great dome, which is 107 feet (32.6m) in diameter and rises to some 180 feet (54.9m) above the floor.

all these early churches was the contrast between their plain exteriors and their glowing interiors. It has been suggested that this reflected a Christian contrast between the matter-of-fact appearance of the material world around us and the glory of the spiritual heaven that is to come.

In 533 Justinian embarked on a reconquest of the by-now barbarian West, and his armies recaptured North Africa from the Vandals and Italy from the Ostrogoths and for a time held part of Spain. The new capital of the reconquered Italy was Ravenna, which could be much more easily

NORTH

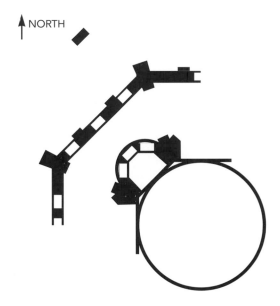

LEFT: Exterior view of San Vitale, Ravenna, Italy. The palace chapel of the emperor Justinian, which was built to commemorate the reconquest of Italy, was consecrated in 547. Though not itself a cathedral, the emperor's chapel became a model for cathedral builders elsewhere.

RIGHT, TOP: Interior view of San Vitale. Note that the interior is richly decorated while the exterior is quite plain.

RIGHT, BOTTOM: Plan of San Vitale. Note that the core of the building is symmetrical, with all chapels and the exterior walls equidistant from the center.

defended than Rome, and Justinian had a number of churches built there. The most notable of these, San Vitale, was domed and centrally planned (symmetrical in all directions), and probably served as the imperial chapel. However, the center of the western Church remained at Rome.

Three years after Justinian's death in 565 a new barbarian tribe, the Lombards, entered Italy and in time conquered much of the peninsula. The Lombard advance threatened the papacy, and in the eighth century the Popes were able to obtain the aid of the Franks, who in turn invaded Italy and conquered the Lombards. The culmination of these events came with the coronation of the Frankish king Charlemagne as emperor on Christmas Day in the year 800, in St. Peter's Cathedral in Rome. We are not sure exactly what the title of emperor meant to Charlemagne. Clearly, he thought of himself as a restorer of Rome, but to a large degree his was the Rome of Byzantine Italy, not the Rome of the old Roman Empire.

When Charlemagne returned to his capital, Aachen (today in Germany), where he was building his new palace, he brought with him marble columns from Ravenna. His palace chapel, the site of his tomb, was modeled on San Vitale, and was domed and centrally planned. By this time the altar was generally placed at the eastern end of the church. One significant Carolingian architectural innovation was the westwork—two stair

13

ABOVE: Mosaic portrait of the emperor Justinian (center, wearing crown) and his court from San Vitale, Ravenna. The richly robed man to the right of the emperor is Archbishop Maximian, who consecrated this church. A similar life-size mosaic portrays the empress Theodora (Justinian's wife) with her court.

OPPOSITE: Interior view of Charlemagne's Palace Chapel at Aachen Cathedral, Rheinland-Pfalz, Germany. The chapel, which was modeled on San Vitale, was consecrated in 805. The octagon is 48 feet (14.6m) in diameter. The view is toward the Gothic choir of the cathedral, which was added between 1355 and 1414. The chandelier was a gift from the emperor Frederick I in 1165.

towers situated on either side of the west entrance to the church. The west-work led to a raised gallery from which the emperor could watch the services below.

During the ninth and tenth centuries, the invasions of the Vikings and the Magyars (Hungarians) helped destroy the unity, prosperity, and cultural revival that had characterized the age of Charlemagne. However, by the early eleventh century, both groups had settled down and had been converted to Christianity. With renewed peace, western Europe began an economic recovery. An early sign of this recovery was what has been called a building boom. New castles, churches, and cathedrals were built throughout

RIGHT: Romanesque arches.

BELOW: An eastward view of the nave at St. Albans Cathedral, Hertfordshire, England. During the Middle Ages, St. Albans was an abbey church; it did not become a cathedral until 1877. The 275-foot (83.8m) Norman nave, which was begun around 1077, is a fine example of a Romanesque interior. Note the paintings on the nave pillars.

OPPOSITE: Mid-thirteenth century depiction of the Last Judgment from the tympanum of the central portal at Bourges Cathedral (Cher), France. The increased emphasis on external decoration can be said to reflect the growing importance given to secular life during this period. Compare this view with that of the exterior of San Vitale.

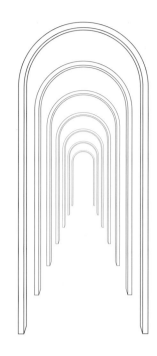

Europe, and a new architectural style—the Romanesque—emerged.

Romanesque architecture was based on Roman models and used materials taken from Roman buildings (when these were available). The styles varied somewhat from region to region, however. In Italy the freestanding bell tower was common; in central Europe churches generally had flat ceilings; in different areas, builders used different kinds of building material, depending upon what was available. The main features that Romanesque churches had in common were the rounded stone vaulting of their

roofs and the massive stone pillars that were required to support the weight of this barrel vaulting. The doors and window arches in Romanesque churches were generally rounded at the top, echoing the shape of the vaults, and there was a new emphasis on exterior decoration, with ornamental carvings around the doors. Over time these ornamental carvings developed to include sculpted portals above the doorways illustrating such religious themes as the Last Judgement or events in the lives of Christ or the Virgin Mary. Some Romanesque churches had twin western towers; some had a semicircular walkway (the ambulatory) around the apse in back of the high altar (the main altar of the church), and this ambulatory gave access to chapels dedicated to particular saints where relics of these saints could be displayed.

By the late eleventh century, builders had begun to modify the Romanesque barrel vault by adding ribs (cross arches) as supports at regular intervals. This technique served to spread the weight of the roof more evenly and created a pleasing pattern in the vault. Next the builders began to replace round arches with pointed ones. The weight of the rounded Romanesque vaults had been borne by thick walls and by the massive columns of the nave. The weight of the pointed vaults rested on the pillars that supported the arched ribs, but to brace these pillars and help overcome the outward thrust on the walls created by the roof's weight, exterior wall supports (buttresses) were built.

At around the same time, builders began to create lighter vaults by using smaller stones set in mortar. Vaults were built higher, and a second type of exterior support, the flying buttress, was developed to carry the thrust from the higher main vaulting over the aisle and ambulatory roofs to the lower supports. As a result of these innovations, heavy walls were no longer necessary to help carry the weight of the roof, and a large part of the wall area could be replaced with stained glass, while the upper range of the cathedral walls (the clerestory) became open stone framing for a series of stained glass windows depicting religious scenes. Stained glass became the main form of interior decoration. The overall effect was an increase of space and light within the church—more than had ever been possible before. The

result of these developments in the art of building is known as Gothic architecture. The abbey church of St.-Denis near Paris, completed in 1144, is considered to be the first Gothic church. From northern France, the Gothic style spread throughout western Europe and came to characterize the cathedrals built or rebuilt over the next three centuries.

In the fifteenth century, the Renaissance style emerged in Italy. Renaissance architecture was based on classical forms. The exteriors of churches were built to resemble ancient temples, the pointed Gothic arch was replaced by a round arch, and the towers and spires of Gothic cathedrals gave way to great domes built on drumlike walls such as those of St. Peter's Cathedral in Rome and St. Paul's Cathedral in London.

Since the Renaissance, a number of new architectural styles have evolved: Baroque (a highly decorated style) developed in the seventeenth and eighteenth centuries, Classical Revival and Gothic Revival in the nineteenth century, and the many styles often lumped together as Modern architecture in the twentieth century. During these periods, however, cathedrals no longer figured among the principal structures being built. Secular building became more important than religious building, and rather than inspiring new types of architecture, new cathedrals simply followed more general building trends.

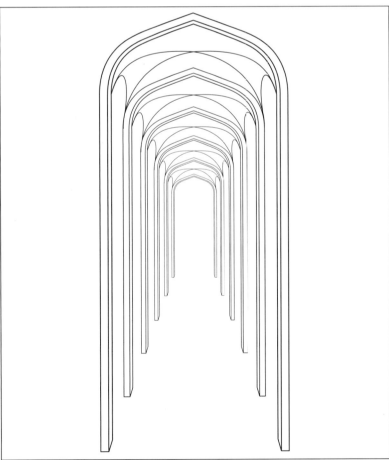

LEFT, TOP: Gothic buttresses at Bourges Cathedral. Flying buttresses carry the thrust of the roof to the buttresses below. Note the three tiers of stained glass and how much of the exterior walling is filled by glass.

LEFT, BOTTOM: Gothic arches.

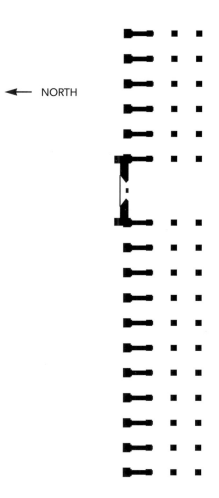

← NORTH

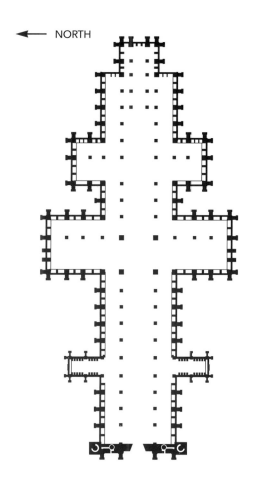

← NORTH

OPPOSITE, TOP: Plan of Notre Dame Cathedral (1150s–c. 1250), Paris (Île-de-France), France.

OPPOSITE, BOTTOM: Plan of Salisbury Cathedral (1220–1258), Wiltshire, England. Note the typically English square east end, the length of the cathedral, and the two sets of transepts. The double square at the lower left marks the north door.

LEFT: The Baroque west front of the Cathedral of Santiago de Compostela in Spain was grafted onto the original Romanesque cathedral between 1738 and 1749.

ABOVE: St. Paul's Cathedral, London, England, was built by Sir Christopher Wren between 1675 and 1710, after the Great Fire of London burned down Old St. Paul's. For more than two centuries, the 365-foot-high (111.3m) dome dominated London's skyline. Note how light is provided by the windows at the base of the dome.

⊕PP⊕SITE: A fine example of a Gothic Revival cathedral, St. Patrick's Cathedral in New York City was built for the most part between 1858 and 1879. The spires were completed in 1888.

AB⊕VE: The Cathedral of Brasília, Brazil, was designed by Oscar Niemeyer and Joachim Cardozo and completed in 1966. The 131-foot (39.9m) reinforced concrete ribs evoke Christ's Crown of Thorns.

BUILDING THE CATHEDRAL AND THE CATHEDRAL'S ROLE

The cathedral played many diverse roles for the community it served. For some, it was a parish church; for all, it was a place of assembly for the great festivities of the church year. Many cathedrals were pilgrimage centers where people went to be cured of illness or to invoke the intercession of the saint or saints whose relics were preserved there. Cathedrals (like churches everywhere but on a grander scale) were sources of religious education. In a world in which most people were illiterate, the stained glass windows, paintings, and sculpture in cathedrals retold the stories, pointed out the lessons, and emphasized the teachings of Christianity. In addition to their religious functions, cathedrals served important social roles. At various times, cathedrals served as meeting places, places of business, storehouses, and fortresses and were also sites of schools, of law courts, and even of sessions of Parliament. Cathedrals were also important markers of social status—to be buried in a cathedral was a sign that your family had "arrived." At the other end of the social scale (and again like churches everywhere), cathedrals provided sanctuary for criminals.

Cathedrals were expressions of the importance and power of the Church as a whole, of the bishop in particular, and of the community in

PAGES 24-25: The cloisters at Norwich Cathedral, Norfolk, England. Norwich's original Norman cloister was destroyed during a town riot against the monks in 1272. These cloisters were built in the fourteenth and fifteenth centuries. Note the roof bosses at the intersections of the vaulting arches.

RIGHT, TOP: Detail of exterior of rose window in the north transept, Cathedral of the Annunciation, Chartres (Eure-et-Loir), France. The north rose at Chartres was donated by the Queen-Regent of France, Blanche of Castile, around 1230.

RIGHT, BOTTOM: Roof boss of the Green Man from the cloisters (early sixteenth century) at Norwich Cathedral. To hold roof vaulting in place, wedge-shaped keystones with flat bases were placed at the intersections of the ribs. Medieval carvers usually decorated the flat undersurface of the keystone with biblical scenes, coats of arms, grotesques, and other figures. Sometimes the bosses were also painted or gilded. This foliate head is of a type thought to originate in pre-Christian fertility worship.

OPPOSITE: Effigies of King Henry IV (r. 1399–1413) and Queen Joan of England at Canterbury Cathedral, Kent, England. Henry had been responsible for the deposition and death of his cousin Richard II and was buried close to the shrine of St. Thomas Becket. According to contemporaries, this was done to seek the martyr saint's intercession.

general. Records, legends, and even panels of stained glass show that members of all classes contributed to the building of cathedrals. Kings, nobles, and bishops were expected to provide support, but merchants, craftsmen, and even peasants contributed as well, though their degree of contribution varied from place to place. At Chartres the guilds donated forty-two stained glass windows, and though Chartres may be an extreme case, it is fair to say that during the Middle Ages cathedrals were an important source of civic pride.

The building of cathedrals to the greater glory of God was a major community undertaking. Cathedrals were built or rebuilt for many reasons. In some cases, bishops moved from smaller to larger cities and built (or started) cathedrals at the new site. Sometimes new cities were raised to episcopal status, requiring the construction of a cathedral. In some cases, structurally sound cathedrals were replaced: new cathedrals were built at Autun, Paris, Florence, and Venice because the older structures were too small, while at Bourges and Laon the older cathedrals were thought to be out of

This detail from Vincent de Beauvais' fifteenth-century illustrated manuscript *Miroir historial* depicts Pope Gregory the Great supervising the building of a church.

date and new cathedrals were built in the current architectural style. In other cases, parts of cathedrals were modified or rebuilt, often for stylistic reasons, but sometimes for liturgical or economic reasons—to provide new chapels or to give greater access to pilgrims.

One major cause for new cathedral building was destruction of an earlier building by fire, earthquake, wind, or war. Most early churches were made of wood; even after cathedrals came to be built of stone, wood continued to be used in the framing and in roof supports. If sparks got under the lead roofing and the wooden beams caught fire, the whole roof could come crashing down into the cathedral below, as happened at Old St. Paul's in London during the Great Fire of 1666. The fire that destroyed the roof of York Cathedral's south transept in 1984 may have been caused by lightning. In the fifty years between 1170 and 1220 there were major cathedral fires at Canterbury, Carlisle, and Chichester in England and at Amiens, Bayonne, Besançon, Chartres, Coutances, Evreux, Reims, Rouen, Strasbourg, and Tours in France. The cathedrals of Constance,

Lincoln, and Naples were damaged by earthquakes. The spires of Lincoln, Old St. Paul's in London, and Troyes and Beauvais in France either blew down or were hit by lightning. Towers fell at Winchester in 1107, at St. David's in 1220, at Lincoln in 1237, at Ely in 1321, and at York in 1407. The roof of Beauvais Cathedral's choir collapsed in 1284, and the central dome of the cathedral of Seville fell in 1511. The cathedrals of Albi, Bari, Béziers, and Rodez were damaged or destroyed by warfare. Repairs and reconstruction might also be needed because of erosion, settling, wood rot, and insect damage.

Cathedral building, however, was very expensive. Building materials sometimes had to be brought from some distance—by water if possible or, if not, most often by oxcart. To reduce the weight to be transported, some materials could be dressed before being brought to the building site, but even so, transport could be difficult and costly. The lantern pillars at Ely that support the octagon are oak beams 63 feet (19.2m) long and roughly three feet (0.9m) thick, and even the smaller supports and trusses were massive by modern standards. To lift such heavy loads, medieval workmen used windlasses and large wheels in which men could walk, but in general work was done by hand, and as many as several hundred workmen might be employed during the building season.

Architectural historian John James has estimated that the cost of rebuilding Chartres between 1194 and 1223 amounted to the equivalent of fifty million dollars—and his estimate has been said to be conservative. In 1976 an appeal was launched for roughly two million dollars to restore the west front of Wells Cathedral in England; the actual cost has been much more. Whatever the modern equivalent of medieval costs, it is clear that cathedral building could stretch the resources of the Church and indeed of the entire community. An additional cost factor was the high quality of both exterior and interior work. Stained glass and carvings set high up in the cathedral's walls or in the vaulting were finished as if they were to be viewed from only a few feet away. Medieval cathedrals were brightly painted, which further added to the expense. Compounding the cost was the attitude of the builders: a cathedral was God's house, and no expense should be spared to beautify it and make it worthy.

As a result of such major (and sometimes unforeseen) expenses, building programs were sometimes launched in moments of civic enthusiasm without adequate long-term funding. A classic example of such a situation is the history of the cathedral at Cologne. When Cologne's fourth-century cathedral was badly damaged by fire in 1248, a new cathedral was begun, although the old cathedral continued to be used for worship. The new cathedral's choir was consecrated in 1322; the unfinished nave was opened for services in 1388; and in 1437 one tower was high enough for a bell to be hung. But then the work slowed, and in 1560 it stopped. Not until the middle of the nineteenth century, at the initiative of the kings of Prussia, was work on the cathedral resumed; finally, in 1880, the cathedral was completed—632 years after its start.

Even when funding was continually available and no interruptions occurred, cathedrals were rarely built in fewer than thirty-five years. Economic slumps, long-term civic declines, changes in donors' priorities, and construction mishaps all served to lengthen the building process. As a consequence, most cathedrals were modified one section at a time. At Canterbury, for example, the original wooden cathedral, built around 600,

Detail of early-thirteenth-century stained glass panel at Chartres Cathedral (Eure-et-Loir), France. This detail from the St. Chéron window shows masons, whose guild donated the window, carving royal sculptures—presumably for a portal.

burned down in 1067. The new Norman stone cathedral was begun in 1070 and was substantially finished by 1107. A fire in 1174 required the choir to be rebuilt between 1175 and 1178, and Trinity Chapel and the Corona were built between 1179 and 1184. The next major period of building took place in the late fourteenth century. Between 1379 and 1405, the now-dilapidated Norman nave was replaced, and over the next fifty years the chapter house (begun a century earlier) was finished, the transepts were remodeled, and the southwest tower and two chapels were built. In 1497 the central tower, begun in the eleventh century, was finally completed, and its vault was finished eight years later. Between 1515 and 1520, Christ Church gate, through which visitors enter the cathedral precinct, was built.

The main source of funding for cathedral building or renovation was income from the lands and property that the cathedral had accumulated through gifts over the centuries. But while these revenues might be sufficient for ordinary building repairs, when rebuilding was needed or substantial new building took place, additional support was necessary. At times like these, individual gifts could be important. In 1202 King John of England (who was then still Duke of Normandy) promised two thousand angevin pounds (roughly 10 percent of his yearly income) to help with the rebuilding of Rouen Cathedral after the fire of 1200.

Grand gifts were exceptional, however. Smaller gifts, such as offerings for individual stained glass windows or altarpieces, were more common. At Chartres, in addition to the windows donated by the guilds, stained glass windows were donated by the queen of France, by several French noble families, by the archbishop

T⊕P: St. Paul's Cathedral, London, England, during a World War II air raid. Although the first five St. Paul's cathedrals on the site were destroyed or badly damaged by fire—in the seventh century, in 961, in 1087, in 1137, and in 1666—the cathedral built by Sir Christopher Wren (between 1675 and 1710) survived the German blitz of 1940 and 1941 and became an international symbol of British resistance.

AB⊕VE: The ruins of Coventry Cathedral, West Midlands, England. Coventry Cathedral was less fortunate than St. Paul's. On November 14, 1940, the late medieval church was destroyed in an air raid by German bombers.

of Canterbury, and by the duke of Brittany, who not only donated several windows but also paid for the statues on the south portal. Taxes of various kinds could also be imposed to support church building. Wren's new St. Paul's was financed in part by a national coal tax, while the building at Notre Dame in Paris during the twelfth and thirteenth centuries was subsidized by a head tax on the serfs on the cathedral's estates. In the twelfth and thirteenth centuries, several cathedrals successfully raised money by sending their relics on tour. In 1272 a number of bishops proclaimed indulgences for those of their subjects who donated to the building of Regensburg Cathedral. At Milan between 1387 and 1392, popular enthusiasm led to gifts of substantial sums of money as well as gifts of labor, and the south tower on the west facade of Rouen Cathedral (built between 1475 and 1507) is known as the "butter tower," supposedly because it was financed by payments from exemptions that allowed people to eat butter during Lent.

In the early days of Christianity, the bishop was often the only full-time clergyman of his church. As time went on, however, congregations grew, new churches were established, and bishops' responsibilities increased, resulting in a growing number of assistants. By the twelfth century, bishops were important figures in both religious and political circles. Bishops often served in royal administrations; in England bishops owed feudal service to the king and sat in the royal councils (as they still do in the House of Lords). Along with their other activities, bishops were often great landowners and sometimes feudal lords of towns.

By this time the bishops' assistants in the clergy were responsible for cathedral services and upkeep, and the sources of revenue for a cathedral

The south side buttresses at Winchester Cathedral, Hampshire, England. Winchester was built in the late eleventh century on a marshy site, and wooden rafts were used to support the walls at the east end. By the late nineteenth century these rafts had rotted, and the walls were in danger of collapsing. New foundations had to be built down to firm gravel—as much as 20 feet (6.1m) below surface level. The buttresses shown here were built in the early part of the twentieth century to brace the cathedral wall.

consisted of regular canons who lived under a semimonastic rule but who could also serve as parish priests. The head of a secular chapter was the dean, and while the bishop might celebrate Easter or Christmas High Mass in the cathedral if he was in residence, the dean often presided over these and other major services of the Church year.

One of the main functions of the clergy of medieval cathedrals was intercession for the dead. In the Middle Ages, most people in the West believed that the prayers of the living could shorten the stay of those who were in purgatory. In cathedrals, as in monasteries, seven prayer services were held daily at regular intervals, in addition to the daily high mass and masses sung at the various other altars of the cathedral. By the fourteenth century, people had begun to establish special chantry chapels in which prayers were to be said forever for the donors and their ancestors. Kings, bishops, nobles, merchants, and guilds established these chantry chapels, which were generally smaller than chapels dedicated to saints and were often built into cathedral walls or between columns in the choir. Old St. Paul's had seventy-four chantry chapels, Laon Cathedral had fifty, and many more prayer endowments were set up under which chantry priests used existing chapels.

Medieval cathedrals and cathedrals today differ in several significant respects; two of these are discussed here. Up until the late Middle Ages, there was no seating in cathedrals and the congregation stood throughout the Mass. While many modern Christians regard the entire cathedral building as sacred, in the Middle Ages only the sanctuary was thought of in this way. This explains such phenomena as the late medieval building of great screens to separate the clergy from the congregation, and the many secular uses that cathedrals were put to. At Old St. Paul's during the fourteenth century, porters used the cathedral as a shortcut, lawyers met their clients there, and public letter writers set up their offices within the cathedral itself. In 1385 Bishop Braybroke threatened to excommunicate "those men and women who daily frequent our cathedral church for the purpose of selling goods," and he went on to censure those boys who played ball both inside and outside the cathedral and who shot arrows and threw stones at pigeons nesting and perching in the walls and porches, to the great damage of the cathedral's sculptures and glass. Perhaps the conclusion to be drawn (though it was certainly not the one the bishop intended) was that in a world where religion was an active and daily part of people's lives, the cathedral was a familiar feature, not just a place one went to a few times a year or visited while on vacation.

were divided between the bishop and the organization of the clergy—the cathedral chapter. There were two main types of cathedral chapter. In England ten of the seventeen medieval cathedrals were monastic cathedrals: the cathedral clergy were monks, had taken monastic vows, and lived in a monastery next to the cathedral. In these cases, the prior of the monastery was head of the chapter and executive officer of the cathedral. On the Continent, secular cathedrals were the norm. Secular clergy of a cathedral (canons) could own property, did not live communally, and did not take vows. Many canons also served as parish priests. An intermediate group

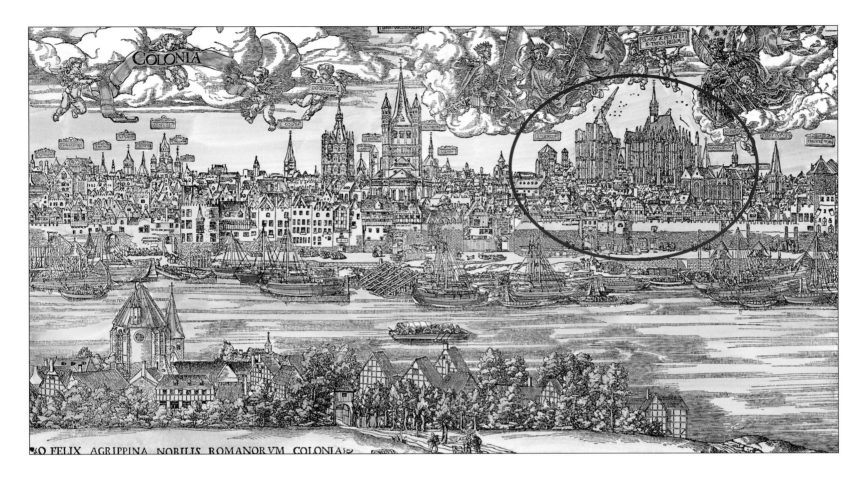

COLONIA

☼O FELIX AGRIPPINA NOBILIS ROMANORVM COLONIA

OPPOSITE: The vault mosaics at St. Mark's Cathedral, Venice, Italy. St. Mark's splendid mosaics in the Byzantine style date from the eleventh to the thirteenth centuries, and cover an area of more than 45,000 square feet (4,185 sq m).

ABOVE: Woodcut showing the city of Cologne, Germany, in 1531, with the unfinished cathedral, begun about three hundred years earlier in 1248, at the upper right. In 1531 the choir had been completed but the west front and the nave would not be finished for another 350 years.

RIGHT: Fragments of a circa-1230 fresco in the Chapel of the Holy Sepulchre at Winchester Cathedral depicting the Deposition and the Entombment. Medieval cathedral interiors were brightly painted, but almost all paintings in areas that adopted Protestantism were destroyed during the Reformation because they were considered to be graven images.

ABOVE: Figures of the Virgin and Child from the west front of Wells Cathedral, Somerset, England. Originally carved in the middle of the thirteenth century, this sculpture was restored in 1970. It is a good example of a detailed and finely finished work that would normally be viewed from a considerable distance.

RIGHT: Vault of the lantern at St. David's Cathedral, Dyfed, Wales. The lower stage of the central tower was built in the thirteenth century, after the previous tower fell in 1220, but the top stage and vault were not completed until the early sixteenth century.

OPPOSITE: Easter High Mass at Westminster Roman Catholic Cathedral, London, England.

ABOVE: Effigy of Bishop William of Wykeham (d. 1404) in his chantry chapel at Winchester Cathedral. Situated between two pillars of the nave, Wykeham's chantry is one of a number of surviving chantry chapels at Winchester. In this chapel a priest would pray daily for the souls of Wykeham and his ancestors.

RIGHT: Winchester Cathedral contains a number of bishops' effigies. This effigy of Bishop Fox (d. 1528), from his chantry chapel, depicts the bishop as a cadaver, rather than as he appeared in life. Such effigies developed in the period after 1346, when recurrent epidemics of the Black Death (bubonic plague) devastated Europe. The effigies served as reminders to the living of the imminence of death and the need for prompt repentance.

C HAPTER T HREE

CATHEDRALS ⊕F GREAT BRITAIN AND IRELAND

Christianity arrived in Britain well before the Christian religion was legalized in the fourth century. During the fifth century, however, Britain was invaded by preliterate, pagan barbarians (the Anglo-Saxons), and where they settled Christianity was wiped out. Christianity survived in the Celtic west of Britain and in Ireland, which was converted during the fifth century.

In 563 Irish monks founded the monastery of Iona on an island just off the southwestern coast of Scotland. From there the monks began to reevangelize northern Britain. In 597 a group of Benedictine monks sent by Pope Gregory the Great landed in southwestern England and soon converted King Ethelbert of Kent. England at the time was divided among a number of tribal kingdoms, and the process of conversion to Christianity often moved from the top down: the king converted first, and his people soon followed. The bishop in each kingdom served as the king's chaplain and established his cathedral in the king's capital. For example, the Roman missionaries led by St. Augustine of Canterbury built their church in Ethelbert's capital at Canterbury.

At a time when populations were small, most of the cathedrals were located on the edges of settlements and were not a part of the town in the

PAGES 38-39: Durham Cathedral, County Durham, England. This magnificent Norman cathedral was built between 1093 and 1133 on a peninsula high above the River Wear. The two 144-foot (43.9m) western towers were built in the late twelfth and early thirteenth centuries; the 218-foot (66.4m) central tower was rebuilt after being struck by lightning in 1429 and 1459. Near the cathedral is the former castle of the bishops of Durham, which today is part of the University of Durham. In 1986 UNESCO (the United Nations Educational, Scientific and Cultural Organization) designated Durham Cathedral and Castle a World Heritage Site.

RIGHT: St.-Peter-on-the-Wall at Bradwell-on-Sea, Essex, England. This church, which was built around 654 by St. Cedd (the first bishop of the East Saxons), served as Cedd's cathedral. It was located on the edge of the Roman fort of Othona, and the builders used quarried Roman building materials. Originally the structure included a semicircular apse, two small transepts, and a porch; the building as a whole was about 82 feet (25m) long. The surviving structure is 24 feet (7.3m) high and roughly 50 feet (15.2m) long, and provides a good sense of how small the earliest English cathedrals were.

way that cathedrals on the Continent were and are. English cathedrals almost always have closes—enclosed grassy areas—around them, while Continental cathedrals are generally built in the midst of cities. Needless to say, the earliest English cathedrals were quite small. Between the seventh century and the Norman Conquest in 1066, a number of changes occurred. Some bishoprics were divided, some were transferred to larger towns; a few new cathedrals were founded, and several older ones disappeared—especially in the areas conquered by the Vikings during the ninth century. In the later Anglo-Saxon period, under the influence of Charlemagne and his successors, some larger English cathedrals were built. Several of these were influenced by Continental buildings—the westwork of the Old Minster at Winchester, for example, was like that of Charlemagne's chapel at Aachen.

The big changes in both the appearance and the organization of English cathedrals came after the Norman Conquest, led by William, Duke of Normandy (later known as William the Conqueror, reigned 1066–1087). One of William's justifications for the invasion was that the archbishop of Canterbury was a usurper, and William took with him a sanctified papal banner. After completing the Conquest, he began replacing Anglo-Saxon bishops with Norman clergy who played an important political role as well as a religious one. William's half-brother Odo, Bishop of Bayeux, served for a time as earl of Kent; the Norman bishop of Durham ruled over a county-palatine in northern England; William's archbishop of Canterbury, Lanfranc of Bec, often acted as regent when William was in

Normandy; and English bishops were responsible for providing the king with knights under the new Norman system of feudalism. The new Norman clergy were involved in monastically inspired and papally led church reform, and a number of the secular Anglo-Saxon cathedral chapters were replaced by monasteries. On the Continent, cathedrals were located within walled towns; a church council held in London in 1075 permitted a number of English bishops to move their sees to larger towns. Over the next few years, bishops moved from Selsey to Chichester, from Litchfield to Chester to Coventry, from Dorchester to Lincoln, from Elmham to Thetford to Norwich, from Sherborne to Sarum, and (for a time) from Wells to Bath. In the first half of the twelfth century, new sees were created at Ely and at Carlisle.

These moves and new diocesan creations led to the construction of new cathedrals. Even where earlier cathedrals already existed, the Normans frequently built new ones. The Normans were prolific builders, and their new cathedrals were generally built on a far grander scale than the Anglo-Saxon structures they replaced. Among the notable characteristics of the Norman cathedrals ("Norman" is used in church architecture to denote the English Romanesque style) were their massive construction, their central towers (sometimes in addition to western towers), their cruciform shape, and their square east ends—in contrast to French cathedrals, where the east end is rounded. Many of the Norman cathedrals were later replaced, wholly or in part, by cathedrals built in the Gothic style. As architectural historian John Harvey has observed, the English cathedrals that remained largely Norman in style were monastic, while most Gothic cathedrals were secular in organization. As Harvey notes, this fact reflected economic trends: at the time the new Gothic style arrived, the balance of wealth within the English Church had shifted from Benedictine monks to the new bishop-administrators.

In England the Gothic architectural period is divided into Early English (c. 1150–1250), Decorated (1250–1350), and Perpendicular (1350–c. 1450). Tudor cathedral architecture (1450–1550) is essentially an extension of Perpendicular. Early English cathedrals are characterized by Gothic pointed arches, lancet windows, more slender columns than those in Norman churches, dog-tooth molding, and simplicity of ornament. Their interiors are much brighter than those of their Romanesque predecessors. The Decorated style is more elaborate, with much naturalistic sculpture. The new skeletal window tracery made possible larger stained glass windows and hence still more light. The Perpendicular style features vertical tracery and interior paneling, large stained glass windows, and splendid English fan vaulting.

The cathedrals at Wells in Somerset and at Salisbury in Wiltshire are excellent examples of the varied conditions under which medieval cathedrals were built and of the common problems experienced by many cathedrals. Both were fortunate enough to escape the major fires that destroyed or badly damaged seven of England's seventeen medieval cathedrals. Both cathedrals were run by secular canons; neither cathedral possessed the shrine of a major saint.

Wells, built between 1175 and 1260, was the first completely Gothic English cathedral. The bishopric of Wells had been created under the Anglo-Saxons in 909, but in 1090 a new French bishop, John de Villula, bought the city of Bath from King William II, and moved his see there. This began a controversy over the proper home of the diocese that lasted for approximately 150 years. Robert, the second bishop following John, established a second throne at Wells, and his successor Reginald FitzJocelin began building a new cathedral there. Reginald's successor Savaric set up yet a third throne at the Abbey of Glastonbury in 1197, and Jocelin, who followed Savaric, styled himself Bishop of Bath and Glastonbury. In 1245 a papal ruling finally established the proper title as Bishop of Bath and Wells, and so it remains. In the meanwhile, the cathedral at Wells grew. Following the usual practice, the church was built from east to west. The choir was built first, so that services could be held, followed by the transepts and the eastern part of the nave. Much of this early work was remodeled in the fourteenth century, but the original plan was basically followed, and the result is unquestionably one of the most beautiful of English cathedrals.

Unlike Wells Cathedral, the Early English cathedral at Salisbury was built on an entirely new site. While Wells was being built, the bishop and canons of (Old) Sarum in Wiltshire decided to move their see. By 1075 the Anglo-Saxon dioceses of Sherborne and Ramsbury had been combined and a new see was then established at Sarum, where there was already a royal castle. Like the castle, the new cathedral and town were sited within the inner ring of a prehistoric hill fort. A building was put up fairly quickly between 1075 and 1092, but shortly after its consecration it was badly damaged by a storm. A new, larger cathedral was built by Bishop Roger and was completed by his death in 1139. By the early thirteenth century, however, a number of problems had arisen: as the town population grew, the limited size of the site led to overcrowding; the water supply was insufficient; and there was constant friction between the clergy and the castle garrison. In 1220 a new cathedral was begun several miles away, at the junction of the Bourne and the Salisbury Avon rivers, and a new planned town—New Sarum, or Salisbury—was built. The cathedral was consecrated

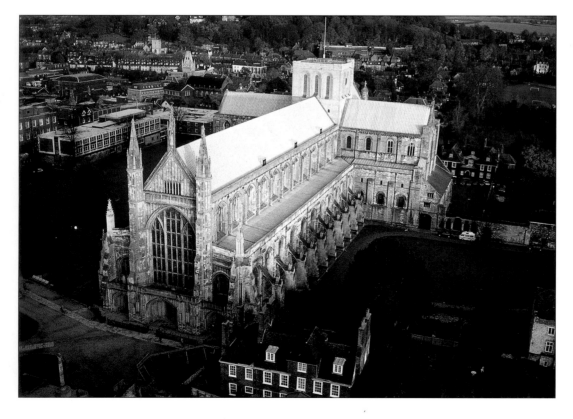

LEFT: Aerial view of Winchester Cathedral, Hampshire, England, from the southwest. The current cathedral was begun in 1079 and consecrated in 1093. The original Norman west front had two transepts and a central tower, and the nave was 40 feet (12.2m) longer than it is today. The west front was rebuilt in the fourteenth century. The present cathedral is 556 feet (169.5m) long—still the longest church in England. Note the modern buttresses on the south side.

OPPOSITE: Detail of the Prior's Door, circa 1135, at Ely Cathedral, Cambridgeshire, England. Note the intricate carving on the door jambs. The Prior's Door, which was close to what was then the prior's lodging, leads from the cloister to the south aisle of the nave. Farther east, close to the site of the former monks' dormitory and refectory, is the less ornate Monks' Door, built during the same period.

in 1258 and has been relatively unchanged since, making Salisbury the only English cathedral constructed in a unified architectural style. The 404-foot (123.1m) spire — now the tallest in England—was added in the fourteenth century as a continuation of an earlier design. Lincoln and Old St. Paul's in London had taller spires than Salisbury's, but the former was blown down in 1548, the latter in 1561.

At both Wells and Salisbury, the piers of the nave and crossing (where nave and transepts meet) were not strong enough to provide adequate support for the weight of the central towers, and in both cases the interiors had to be reinforced. At Wells the solution was the dramatic scissor arches that brace the pillars at the crossing. Scissor arches were also constructed at Salisbury, but these were only extensions of the choir; arches were not built at right angles to the nave as at Wells. Later, strainer arches had to be added for further support. Nevertheless, the spire today leans almost two and a half feet (0.8m) to the southwest.

From the twelfth century on, a good deal of cathedral rebuilding took place. The interiors of Norman cathedrals were made lighter by the addition or enlargement of stained glass windows, as at Norwich and Peterborough (a Norman abbey church that became a cathedral in 1541). Cloisters were rebuilt everywhere. Various new architectural features were developed in the twelfth and thirteenth centuries, including chapter houses,

where the cathedral clergy met, and Lady Chapels, which were one result of the growing liturgical devotion to the Virgin Mary. The growing competence of builders led them to put up higher vaults than before, and although the vaulting never reached the heights of some European cathedrals, English cathedrals tended to have longer naves than their Continental counterparts. As on the Continent, for most of the Middle Ages the primary goals of medieval English cathedral builders were to increase both space and light to the greater glory of God.

The Protestant Reformation brought about a number of changes for English cathedrals. In 1533, after he had been unable to get papal dispensation for a divorce from Catherine of Aragon in order to marry Anne Boleyn, Henry VIII broke with Rome and declared himself Supreme Head of the Church of England. In 1539 the greater monasteries (those with incomes of more than two hundred pounds per year) were taken over by Henry and their buildings and property were confiscated. The former monastic cathedrals were turned over to secular canons, monastic libraries and treasuries were looted, and in some cases monastic buildings were demolished or converted to other uses. Of the cathedral churches, Coventry and Bath were stripped: the shell of the former was eventually destroyed; a portion of the latter was in time salvaged. In the early 1540s, to meet the needs of a growing population, Henry had six former monastic churches raised to cathedral status—Bristol, Chester, Gloucester, Oxford, Peterborough, and Westminster (which remained a cathedral for only ten years).

The new Anglican Church, as it evolved under Henry, his son Edward VI, and his daughter Elizabeth I, continued to follow many of the observances of the medieval Church, but the cathedrals were no longer the community focus they had been. During the sixteenth and seventeenth centuries, many cathedrals suffered damage at the hands of Protestant extremists. When they could, the Puritans pulled down or damaged the sculptures and effigies they could reach, broke stained glass windows, and whitewashed painted interiors. In 1650 Durham Cathedral was used as a prison for defeated Scots; because there was no heat in the cold stone cathedral, the prisoners broke up the cathedral woodwork for their fires. Up to the nineteenth century, the only new cathedral constructed in England was St. Paul's in London, built by Wren after the Great Fire of 1666.

By the eighteenth century, many English medieval cathedrals were in need of repair, and by the end of the century James Wyatt, the first prominent cathedral "restorer," was at work. Wyatt is a controversial figure: he has

A westward view of the nave of Durham Cathedral. Note the alternating compound piers and massive circular columns—the Norman columns in the foreground are decorated with zigzag ornament. Note also the ribbed cross vault with the earliest pointed arches (1128–1133) in any English cathedral.

been called the equivalent of an architectural butcher, but he has also been said to be "misunderstood." While Wyatt did help to preserve parts of some cathedrals, he certainly damaged others, in some cases irreparably (he took three inches [7.6 cm] of stone off the exterior of Durham Cathedral), and many of his "restorations" were redone during the nineteenth century. The Gothic Revival brought with it a new wave of restorers, and their attempts to create "purified" Gothic cathedrals according to an ideal "Gothic" pattern produced a new wave of critics.

The population explosion of the nineteenth century led to the creation of a number of new bishoprics. In most cases parish churches were

raised to cathedral status—a trend that has continued in the twentieth century. Several Anglican cathedrals have been built during this century. The cathedrals at Guildford and Liverpool, both entirely new churches that do not replace older buildings, are traditional, architecturally conservative buildings, but in Coventry a dramatic modern cathedral was built to replace the medieval church destroyed in a bombing raid during World War II.

In 1850, after restrictions on Roman Catholic worship had been lifted, thirteen Catholic bishoprics were founded. The most spectacular of the Catholic cathedrals that were built as a result is Westminster Cathedral in London, begun in 1895 in the Byzantine style and built of brick. It should be noted that while most English cathedrals are either Anglican or Roman Catholic, London also has Greek and Ukrainian cathedrals.

By and large, Welsh, Scottish, and Irish cathedrals were built on a more modest scale than the great English cathedrals. Wales was a poorer area than England, and its four medieval cathedrals were among the most poorly endowed in Britain. The finest of these, St. David's in Dyfed, contained the shrine of St. David, the patron saint of Wales, who is said to have founded the cathedral around 550. The present cathedral was begun in the twelfth century. Next to it are the ruins of a splendid bishop's palace whose lead roof was stripped off during the Reformation.

Scotland, too, was less prosperous and less populous than England, though southern lowland Scotland had a number of fine medieval cathedrals. However, the Scottish Protestants were more numerous and more radical, on the whole, than the English. During the sixteenth century, many Scottish cathedrals were destroyed, and all were damaged. A few

were preserved, largely because the Scottish sovereigns, Mary Queen of Scots and her son James VI, were able to maintain Episcopalian bishops despite the fact that most Scots were Presbyterians, but in 1690 the Church of Scotland finally became Presbyterian. Those cathedrals that survived were used as parish churches. In the second half of the nineteenth century, after laws repressing Episcopalian and Roman Catholic worship had been repealed, several new Scottish Episcopalian and Roman Catholic cathedrals were built.

Ireland experienced a relatively late conversion to Christianity during the fifth century, at a time when no towns had as yet developed. Conversion of the Irish clans was accomplished by monastic missionaries, and the Irish church was organized along monastic rather than episcopal lines, with Irish abbots ranking above bishops. In the twelfth century, the Irish church was reorganized, and by 1200 thirty-six dioceses had been created. For the most part the bishops were located in towns that were still quite small. Some new cathedrals were built starting in the thirteenth century, but most medieval Irish cathedrals were small—no larger than many English parish churches—in keeping with the populations they served.

At the Reformation, the great majority of the Irish people remained Roman Catholic, but since Ireland was under English control, the established church became Protestant, and services were held in the English language. During the seventeenth and eighteenth centuries, new cathedrals were built at Londonderry (now Derry), Cashel, and Waterford, while cathedrals at Lismore and Dromore were rebuilt. In the nineteenth and twentieth centuries, more than twenty new Roman Catholic cathedrals were built to replace those taken over by Protestants at the Reformation, while new Church of Ireland (Protestant) cathedrals were built at Belfast, Cork, Ferns, and Kilmore, and more than a dozen older cathedrals were restored.

View of St. Hugh's Choir. looking west, at Lincoln Cathedral, Lincolnshire, England. St. Hugh's Early English Choir was built after an earthquake in 1185 had damaged the Norman east end. The choir stalls, circa 1365–1370, were donated by the cathedral treasurer John of Welborn and retain most of their medieval carvings.

LEFT: View of the choir, looking east, at Canterbury Cathedral, Kent, England. After the Norman choir at Canterbury burned in 1174, the monks brought in a French architect, William of Sens, to build a new choir as a setting for the shrine of St. Thomas Becket, who had been martyred in the cathedral four years earlier. William of Sens introduced the Gothic style to English cathedrals, and in 1179 he was crippled by a fall from a scaffold. He was replaced by William the Englishman, who completed Trinity Chapel, the choir in which the shrine was placed; the ambulatory through which pilgrims walked to view the shrine; and the Corona, with its stained glass windows. As in other cases where great shrines were built behind the high altar, the bishop's throne was moved, here to the south side of the choir. In 1220, on the fiftieth anniversary of Becket's martyrdom, the saint's body was moved into its splendid new tomb, where it remained until the tomb was stripped and destroyed at the order of Henry VIII.

BELOW: Detail of Canterbury Cathedral's Trinity Chapel Miracle Window VII depicting the story of Adam the Forester. Stained glass windows in Trinity Chapel depicted miracles performed by Becket after his martyrdom. Here Adam the Forester is shot in the neck by a poacher, is cured by drinking water from St. Thomas's Well (where the saint had bled), and gives thanks at the saint's tomb. Both the stained glass windows and the raised position of the gold-plated shrine should be thought of in terms of stage management: they created a theatrical setting that helped make Canterbury one of the most popular pilgrimage destinations in Europe and brought substantial revenues to the monks of the cathedral.

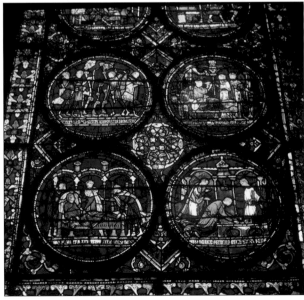

VE: View of the nave, looking east, at Peterborough Cathedral, Cambridgeshire, England. Peterborough was an abbey until , when it became a cathedral church. The present building replaced an earlier structure ravaged by fire in 1116. The Norman is crowned by a painted wooden ceiling constructed around 1220. This ceiling is unique in England, and is one of only a few surviving in Europe.

AB☯VE: The west front of Wells Cathedral, Somerset, England, was built circa 1230–1260. This facade is a gallery of some of the finest surviving sculpture from thirteenth-century England. The 147-foot-wide (44.8m) facade has six tiers of statues. Originally there were some four hundred figures, each of which was brightly painted. Many of these statues were destroyed by Puritans in the seventeenth century and many have been damaged by corrosion; today only about three hundred remain. The statues have been restored several times. The two towers date from the late fourteenth and fifteenth centuries.

RIGHT: The chapter house steps at Wells Cathedral. Wells' chapter house, completed circa 1310, is unusual in that it was built above ground level. The elegant staircase leading from the eastern aisle of the north transept to the chapter house doorway at right center continues up to a fifteenth-century passage leading to the vicars' hall. Note how the staircase is illuminated by the windows on the left.

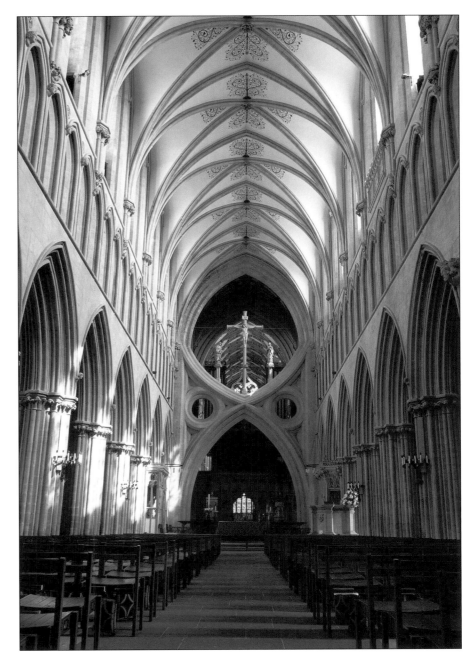

ABOVE: View of the nave at Wells, looking east. Soon after the central tower was completed in 1322, it began to tilt to the west, the piers of the crossing sank, and cracks developed in the walls. The solution to these problems was the insertion of the dramatic scissor arch across the far end of the nave, with two similar arches spanning the crossing at the sides.

LEFT: View of Salisbury Cathedral, Wiltshire, England, from the northeast. Salisbury was built between 1220 and 1258 on a new site soon after it was decided to move the cathedral from an earlier location two miles (3.2km) away. Salisbury is the only English cathedral to survive in a uniform architectural style (Early English). Its 404-foot (123.2m) spire can be seen for many miles.

ABOVE: View of the choir at Salisbury Cathedral from the nave. At the upper left and right are the strainer arches that help support the weight of the tower. The darker shafts of the piers are made from a variety of English stone known as Purbeck marble. Note the square east end with the Lady Chapel beyond.

RIGHT: Exterior view of the lantern at Ely Cathedral, Cambridgeshire, England. In 1322 the Norman central tower at Ely collapsed. Ely's famous octagonal lantern—a Gothic central tower that provided light to the crossing—was built in its place, following a plan by the monk Alan of Walsingham.

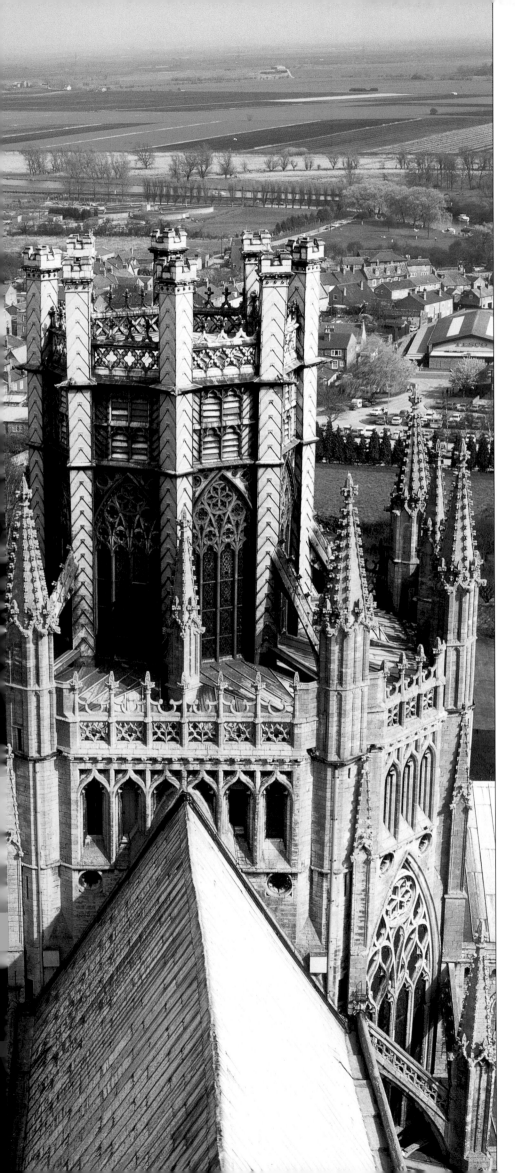

AB✛VE: Interior view of Ely Cathedral's octagon. At the center is Christ giving a blessing, encircled by angels. The octagon at Ely is one of the finest features of any cathedral in the world.

BEL✛W: View of Old St. Paul's, London, England, from the south, before 1561. The fourth cathedral on the site was begun in 1087 and was not finished until about 1285. Old St. Paul's 586-foot (178.6m) nave was then the longest of any English cathedral, and its steeple and tower were 493 feet (150.3m) high, second only to Lincoln. The steeple was struck by lightning and burned in 1561; the cathedral itself was destroyed by the Great Fire of London in 1666.

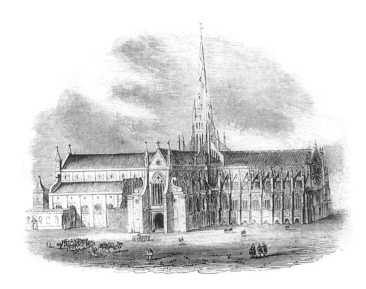

ABOVE: The south walk of the great cloister at Gloucester Cathedral, Gloucestershire, England. In 1377 Abbot Horton began a complete rebuilding of the Norman cloisters—a reconstruction not completed until 1412. The cloisters contain the earliest fan vaulting in England, and the south walk has twenty carrels (left), each of which could be equipped with a desk at which a monk could study or write. The north walk contains the lavatorium where the monks washed up.

LEFT: Exterior view of the east end at York Cathedral. York has the finest surviving collection of stained glass of any English cathedral; its glory is the east window, designed and installed by John Thornton between 1405 and 1408. This window is 76 feet 9 inches (23.4m) high and 32 feet (9.8m) wide—the largest single surviving medieval stained glass window. It portrays, from the top down, God as alpha and omega, angels, patriarchs, Old Testament heroes, prophets, saints, scenes from the Old Testament, scenes from the Book of Revelation, and at the bottom, a row of English saints, kings, archbishops of York, and the donor, Bishop Skirlaw of Durham. The east end of the cathedral is essentially a skeletal frame for the window.

ABOVE: View from the nave toward the choir screen and choir, York Cathedral, North Yorkshire, England. The choir screen was completed in the second half of the fifteenth century to support the eastern piers of the crossing and to separate the nave from the choir. The screen is decorated with life-size statues of fifteen English kings. Where such screens were built, the high altar was hidden from the view of the congregation and a nave altar was provided for the use of the laity.

ABOVE: The Cathedral of St. Michael, Coventry, West Midlands, England. The present cathedral was built between 1954 and 1962 after the medieval parish church that had served as the cathedral since 1918 was destroyed during a World War II air raid. The bronze sculpture of St. Michael overcoming the devil is by Sir Jacob Epstein.

RIGHT: Westminster Cathedral, London, England, was designed by John Francis Bentley in the Byzantine style; it was begun in 1895 and consecrated in 1910. Its striking appearance is due in part to alternating bands of red brick and gray Portland stone. The bell tower is 284 feet (86.6m) high. The interior, whose decoration is still not completed, contains mosaics, sculptures, and colored marbles from all over the world.

ABOVE: The ruins of St. Andrews Cathedral, Fife, Scotland. Around 1160, at a time when the Scottish kings were trying to make St. Andrews the seat of an archbishopric, a new cathedral was begun, but it was not consecrated until 1318. The cathedral was 335 feet (102.1m) long—the largest in Scotland. Although it was damaged during the Reformation, the final ruin of the cathedral was brought about by disuse, neglect, and local townsmen's subsequent quarrying of the structure for building materials.

RIGHT: St. Colman's Roman Catholic Cathedral, Cobh (pronounced "Cove"), County Cork, Republic of Ireland, was designed by E.W. Pugin and G. Ashlin and built between 1868 and 1919. This neo-Gothic cathedral, with its 300-foot (91.4m) spire, is situated atop a steep 150-foot (45.7m) hill overlooking the harbor.

BELOW: The nave at St. David's Cathedral, Dyfed, Wales. The present cathedral with its late Norman nave was built between 1180 and 1198. The screen separating the nave from the choir dates from the second quarter of the fourteenth century and contains the tomb of Bishop Henry Gower, who had the screen built. The wooden ceiling with its hanging pendants was contructed around 1500.

CHAPTER FOUR

CATHEDRALS OF FRANCE, BELGIUM, AND SPAIN

Under the Romans, Gaul (which included the area that is now France) consisted essentially of three different parts. To the south, along the Mediterranean coast, was an urbanized area that had been colonized by Greeks long before its conquest by Rome in the second century B.C. North of this was an agricultural area whose scattered cities were for the most part founded after Julius Caesar's conquest of Gaul in 58–51 B.C. The third part of Gaul was the frontier area along the Rhine, which today is part of Germany. Christianity seems to have taken hold first in the Greek-speaking coastal cities and gradually spread inland. Many of the important non-coastal Gallic cities were located on rivers, and Christian communities—and cathedrals—tended to be clustered along these waterways.

During the fifth century A.D., Gaul suffered invasions by a number of barbarian tribes. The Vandals and Visigoths had been converted to a heretical form of Christianity before they entered Roman territory. Clovis, first king of a united Frankish people, converted to orthodox Christianity soon afterward, in 486. The Church was therefore preserved by the barbarian invaders of Gaul not destroyed as in Britain. The Franks were essentially a rural people and Clovis's successors degenerated into what have been called the "do-nothing" kings. As a result, the cities of Gaul declined both in population and in prosperity, and their bishops often became their effective rulers. Gallic cathedrals built at this time were generally small, as was the case in other parts of the West.

The Carolingians, a new dynasty whose first king, Pepin the Short (reigned 751–768), was succeeded by Charlemagne (r. 768–814), were able to reassert royal control for a time, but during the ninth century civil wars, land divisions, and Viking raids led to the end of any effective central authority. To protect against the Vikings, as well as against raiding Magyars (Hungarians) and Arabs, many cities were fortified. By the late tenth century, when the invaders were either settled or had been defeated, the typical French cathedral lay within a walled town whose lord was often the bishop of the area. The Romanesque style of building that developed during this period can be said to have been given an important impetus by Charlemagne, who set out to revive Roman culture and introduced to

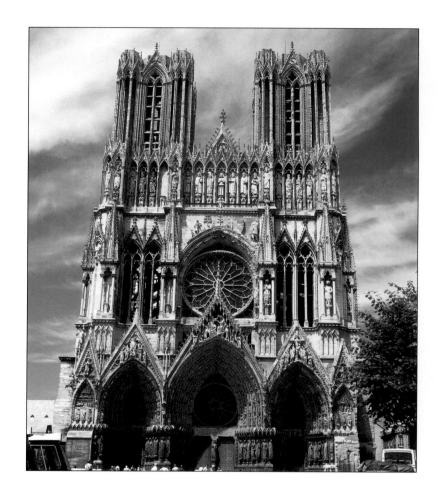

PAGES 60–61: Interior view of the lantern at the crossing of the nave and transepts, Cathedral of Notre-Dame, Coutances (Manche), France. See page 64 for more information.

RIGHT, TOP: The west front of the Cathedral of Notre-Dame, Reims (Marne), France. Reims was begun in 1211, roughly sixty years after Paris, and by comparing the two west fronts, some of the stylistic developments that occurred during the intervening period can be seen. The front of Reims is generally more elaborate. While there are some round arches on the upper levels of the cathedral in Paris, all the arches at Reims are pointed. Note the two rose windows in Reims' facade and the extensions above the portals. In the middle extension the Coronation of the Virgin is depicted. The cathedral at Reims was the coronation church of the French kings.

RIGHT, BOTTOM: The west front of the Cathedral of Notre-Dame, Paris (Île-de-France), France. Notre-Dame was begun in the 1150s to replace a small Romanesque cathedral. The great size of the new cathedral resulted from the position of Paris as the main town (soon to be the capital) of the rising Capetian kings of France. The twin towers are 215 feet (65.5m) high. Below the great west rose window, which measures 30 feet (9.1m) in diameter, are statues of the kings of Judah and Israel; below them are the three western portals—from left to right, the Portal of the Virgin, the Portal of the Last Judgment, and the Portal of St. Anne— named after the sculptures on the tympanum of each doorway.

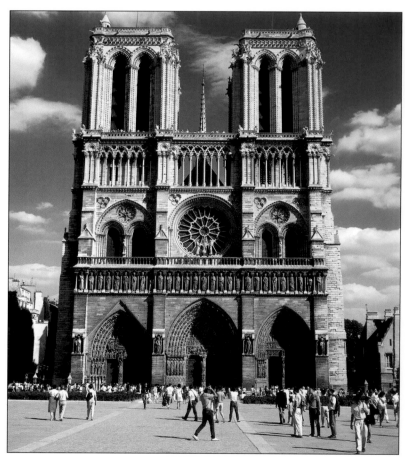

62

ABOVE: The west tower of the Cathedral of Notre-Dame, Laon (Aisne), France. In 1112 the burghers of Laon revolted against their feudal lord, the bishop. The resultant fire damaged the cathedral, and although repairs were made, a new Gothic cathedral was begun in mid-century and was largely completed some seventy years later. Laon is located on a hill above a large plain and teams of oxen had to drag building stones for the cathedral up the steep hill. The sculptures of sixteen oxen on the twin towers are said to commemorate those oxen and a miracle that occurred when one day an ox collapsed and was replaced by another that suddenly appeared, finished hauling the load to the site, and then vanished.

northern Europe the elements of Byzantine architecture. But until order was restored, the amount of new building was necessarily limited.

The revival of Europe that took place in the eleventh and twelfth centuries (and somewhat earlier in Germany) was a complex process. Greater political order led to a revival of trade and commerce, and an expanding population led to territorial expansion and to the physical growth and greater prosperity of cities. Increased contact with the Byzantine and Islamic worlds led to a greater demand for education. Accompanying this secular revival was a simultaneous growth in religious fervor. Laymen had appointed and sold church offices and sometimes assumed such offices themselves. The monastery of Cluny (founded in 910) attempted to free

the Church from the secular control under which it had fallen during the ninth- and tenth-century breakdown of central authority and the rise of feudalism. By the eleventh century, the ideals of Cluny had reached the papacy, which freed itself from control by the German emperors and sought to reform the Church everywhere. Bishops benefited from many of these developments: they were able to regain control over their sources of income, they ruled over growing populations, their towns became more prosperous, and the cathedral schools, particularly those in northern France, became centers for an intellectual revival. As reform spread from the monasteries to the nonmonastic church, donations to the cathedrals by those seeking the prayers of cathedral clergy increased. All these events brought more money into cathedral treasuries, and the increased revenue led in turn both to new building and to rebuilding of cathedrals in the new Romanesque style.

The earliest Romanesque churches were built in southern France, Spain, and northern Italy in the late tenth century. By the turn of the eleventh century, the style had spread north, moving along the river valleys. Each region developed its own version of the Romanesque style based on a particular combination of tradition and local building materials. New buildings went up everywhere. As the monk Raoul Glaber wrote of the time immediately after the year 1000: "Christians competed with one another in renewing their churches in a more elegant style. It was as if the world…, throwing off the old, was everywhere clothing itself in a white robe of churches. Then the faithful improved almost all the cathedrals, as well as monasteries dedicated to various saints, and even the little village chapels."

During the late tenth century, a major cathedral school developed at Chartres under Fulbert, a famous master who later became bishop. In 1020 Fulbert began a new cathedral after its predecessor, built some fifty years before, was destroyed by fire. Like that of other Romanesque churches, Chartres' design was influenced by changes in religious practice—notably by the increased veneration of relics and the greater number of masses celebrated, and in particular by masses said for souls in purgatory. These developments led to increases in the size of crypts (to house shrines and provide pilgrims with access to them) and in the number of chapels and altars. The new Romanesque cathedral at Chartres had three crypt chapels as well as radiating chapels at the east end. Similar arrangements developed at Auxerre and Nevers, both of whose Romanesque cathedrals were built at about the same time as Chartres. In all, from the late tenth to the early twelfth century more than forty new French Romanesque cathedrals were built (many after fires), and nine others were reconstructed. Many of these Romanesque buildings were later replaced by cathedrals in the Gothic style.

The Romanesque style developed more or less simultaneously throughout western Europe. The Gothic style originated in northern France; more precisely, the elements that made up the Gothic style came together there. From the twelfth to the mid-fourteenth century, the French population continued to grow, reaching a peak not equaled again until the eighteenth century; population growth led in turn to economic growth, accompanied by political consolidation. Starting with Philip Augustus (r. 1179–1223), the Capetian kings expanded royal authority over most of feudal France. By the time of Louis IX's death in 1270, France was the best governed and most prosperous country in Europe. Along with this economic and political growth went a brilliant cultural advance. Paris was the site of northern Europe's first university and the center for philosophic studies from the time of Abelard in the early twelfth century to that of Albertus Magnus and Thomas Aquinas in the thirteenth century. During the same period, French vernacular literature (from poetry and Arthurian romances to historical writing) flourished; major developments were made in polyphonic music; and France saw not only the origin but also what has been called the "perfection" of Gothic architecture.

The first Gothic church, Saint Denis (then in a suburb of Paris), was completed in 1144. By the mid-twelfth century, new cathedrals incorporating Gothic elements were under construction at Sens, Senlis, and Noyon. However, the explosion in Gothic cathedral building can be said to have begun in the 1160s. Between the second half of the twelfth century and the middle of the thirteenth century, more than twenty-five French cathedrals were begun or reconstructed in the Gothic style, including

ABOVE: Interior view of the lantern of the central tower, Cathedral of Notre-Dame, Coutances (Manche), France, built in the second quarter of the thirteenth century. Between 1210 and 1250 (interrupted by a fire in 1218), the Romanesque cathedral at Coutances was modernized in the Gothic style. One of Coutances' finest features is this lantern, which rises some 134 feet (40.8m) above the cathedral floor.

OPPOSITE: The cathedral of Notre-Dame at Paris is famous for its gargoyles. They appear at the ends of waterspouts or freestanding (as here). It has been suggested that such figures of evil spirits were designed to frighten away real evil spirits. The present gargoyles date from the nineteenth-century restoration of the cathedral.

Amiens, Chartres, Paris, Reims, and Strasbourg — some of the most famous cathedrals in any architectural style.

The circumstances under which these cathedrals were built varied greatly: at Paris the bishops and royal officials were major givers; at Amiens the local clergy made important contributions to the work; and at Chartres and Strasbourg the townspeople played a vital role. Some cathedrals were largely complete within a relatively short period of time—Amiens and Reims in fifty years; Chartres, Laon, Paris, and Strasbourg in less than a century. The towers usually took longer to finish: Amiens' two towers took an additional 130 years to complete, Reims' took two hundred years in all, and Strasbourg's north tower was never finished. At Chartres the north spire was hit by lightning in 1506; as a result, this cathedral has two spires built 350 years apart.

Many of the differences between Romanesque and Gothic cathedrals have already been discussed. With the great increase in the amount of stained glass, rose windows became a common feature. Romanesque cathedrals had sculptured portals and tympana (semicircular arches above the doorways), and the usual subject depicted on the tympanum of the central portal of the west entrance was the Last Judgment. Gothic sculptors expanded the range of subjects on the tympanum and introduced statues on the columns supporting the tympanum and flanking the doors. The tympana of Gothic cathedrals show scenes from the lives of Christ, the Virgin, and various saints. A frequent subject was the Coronation of the Virgin, reflecting the growing veneration of the Virgin during the thirteenth century. Statues included Old and New Testament figures, prophets, martyrs, confessors, virgins, popes, kings, and queens. At Chartres the martyrs stand on their persecutors, and arch moldings display the Labors of the Months, the liberal arts, and various crafts. At Paris one finds scenes of university life and of the torments of hell. The portals, like

ABOVE: Upper part of the exterior of the south portal at the Cathedral of Saint Pierre, Beauvais (Oise), France, built during the first half of the sixteenth century. Beauvais' choir collapsed in 1284. The damage was repaired over the next forty years, but building then stopped for almost two centuries. The nave was never built; only the choir stands. The south portal, completed in 1548, was built in the Late Gothic Flamboyant style.

OPPOSITE: The royal portal, circa 1145–1155, of the Cathedral of the Assumption, Chartres (Eure-et-Loir), France. The west portal, built after a fire in 1134, was influenced by the portal at Saint-Denis. The south tympanum (right) depicts the Virgin and Child; below are scenes from the life of the Virgin and the infancy of Christ; and on the archivolts are representations of the seven liberal arts. The north tympanum depicts the ascension of Christ below the symbols of the zodiac and the "Labors of the Months"—occupations associated with the months of the year. In the central tympanum is Christ in Glory surrounded by the symbols of the evangelists. Below are the apostles, and on the archivolts are angels and elders of the Apocalypse. The statues on the door jambs—Old Testament figures—are thought to represent the ancestors of Christ.

the stained glass windows, became theaters for depicting the teachings of the Church, the rhythms of life, and the working of God in the universe. A tendency developed everywhere to view the figures as part of an overall conception: the figures on the columns are related to the scene on the tympanum, while the figures on the moldings often depict the heavenly hierarchy. One can see in the portals, and indeed throughout the Gothic cathedrals, the same organized thought that was also manifested in the great thirteenth-century philosophic encyclopedias.

Along with stylistic changes came some liturgical and structural changes. The movement of the shrines of saints from the crypt to the area behind the high altar ended the building of large crypts. The greater number of clergy participating in the Mass resulted in the lengthening of the

choirs. The most dramatic change, however, came about for competitive reasons. For a period of a hundred years, the heights of cathedral vaults steadily rose. In the 1170s the vault at Notre-Dame in Paris was 108 feet high (32.9m); twenty years later at Chartres the height was 120 feet (36.6m); in the 1220s Amiens' vault was 139 feet (42.4m) high; and finally at Beauvais, in the 1270s, the vault reached 157 feet (47.9m) in height. In 1284, however, the vault at Beauvais collapsed, and the race was over.

Cathedral building or reconstruction was often determined by historical events—in particular by war and civil uprisings. In the twelfth century, southern France became a center for the heretical sect known as the Cathari, or Albigensians. In 1208, after the murder of a papal legate, Pope Innocent III proclaimed a crusade against the Albigensians. In the crusade's first year, the city of Béziers was sacked, and according to one estimate seven thousand people were burned alive when the crusaders set fire to the cathedral. The cathedral at Albi was also badly damaged during the crusade, which dragged on for some twenty years. In the after-

ABOVE: Stained glass in the west portal of Chartres Cathedral. The west rose window, circa 1215, represents the Last Judgment. The three mid-twelfth-century windows below (viewed from right to left) depict the Tree of Jesse (a pictorial representation of Isaiah's prophesy), Christ's Incarnation, and His Passion and Resurrection, echoing the themes on the west portal on the exterior side of the wall.

Noyon, Soissons, and Verdun. The cathedral at Chalons was bombarded again in 1940 and 1944, and Nevers, Rouen, and Saint-Malo were bombed in 1944. Yet all these structures have been restored!

Belgian and Spanish cathedrals were significantly influenced by French cathedral architecture. The area that is now Belgium was within the northern frontier area of Roman Gaul and was later conquered by the Franks. After the death of the emperor Louis I in 840, the Frankish territory was subdivided several times. The area that later became modern Belgium was divided between France and Germany and remained so divided for most of the Middle Ages. The area was also divided linguistically (as it is today) between those who spoke French and those who spoke Flemish, a West German language related to Dutch. During the eleventh century, the entire area experienced great prosperity as a result of the growth of a cloth-making industry. Among the major towns that rose during this period were Bruges, Ghent, and Ypres. In the fifteenth century, Antwerp became one of the most important cities of the area, owing in good measure to the silting-

math, Languedoc came under Capetian control and under the supervision of the Inquisition. When the cathedrals at Béziers and Albi were rebuilt, they were constructed for defensive as well as spiritual purposes. During the fourteenth and fifteenth centuries, France experienced the ravages of the Hundred Years' War and of the Black Death epidemic, and construction everywhere slowed or stopped. As early as 1346, the English sacked the cathedrals at Poitiers and Saint-Brieuc. During the sixteenth-century Wars of Religion, the Huguenots (French Protestants) destroyed the cathedral of Pamiers, sacked the cathedral of Agde, set the cathedral of Orléans on fire, and on two occasions badly damaged the cathedral of Sées. In the French Revolution, many cathedrals were badly damaged or vandalized. A good deal of the stained glass of the cathedral of Strasbourg was damaged during the siege of that city in the Franco-Prussian War (1870). During World War I, a number of cathedrals were shelled, including Chalons-sur-Marne,

up of the river at Bruges and the subsequent decline of that city.

Belgian cities were subject to nobles such as the counts of Flanders, the dukes of Brabant, and from the late fourteenth century, the dukes of Burgundy. These cities had their own militias and a good deal of independence, and at times were at war with their feudal lords. Belgian cities were characterized by a great deal of local pride, which manifested itself in the building of cathedrals and great town halls and guild halls. From the fourteenth to the sixteenth century, Belgian church towers grew taller and taller, though some were cut short before reaching their projected heights.

Spain was conquered by the Romans well before Christianity spread there. During the fifth century, Iberia (as Spain and Portugal were then known) was conquered by the Visigoths. At the time the Visigoths were Arian heretics, but they later converted to orthodox Christianity. In 711 Moslems from North Africa crossed the Strait of Gibraltar and within eight years had conquered most of the Iberian peninsula. The Moslems (or Moors, as they were often called) remained in Spain for more than seven hundred years and had a major influence on Spanish history and culture. Christian Spanish territory was reduced to a narrow strip in the mountainous north and west. In the ninth century, a tomb supposed to be that of St. James (Santiago) the Apostle to Spain was found in the city of Compostela in northwestern Spain. Santiago the Moorslayer became the champion of Christian resistance against the Moors. By the tenth century, the Christian reconquest (Reconquista) had begun—a long process that concluded with the expulsion of the Moors from their last stronghold, Granada, in 1492. In the twelfth century, the kingdom of Portugal was founded; but over time, the other small kingdoms on the peninsula became united through marriage, and in 1479 the marriage of Ferdinand II of Aragon and Isabella of Castile led finally to a unified Spain.

In general the surviving Spanish cathedrals were built relatively late, often after cities had been reconquered from the Moors. One can see a strong French architectural influence in some Spanish cathedrals, but there was also a significant Moorish influence. During the sixteenth century, Charles I (who became the emperor Charles V) inherited Spain from his mother and the possessions of the dukes of Burgundy from his father, and ruled as well over the rich Spanish Empire in the New World. Consequently, Spain became the great European power of that time. With this legacy of wealth and power available to support the development of art and architecture, Charles's reign saw the beginning of the Golden Age of Spanish Painting as well as a great deal of building, and during the seventeenth and eighteenth centuries exteriors in the ornate Baroque style were applied to a number of Spanish cathedrals that had been built in earlier architectural styles.

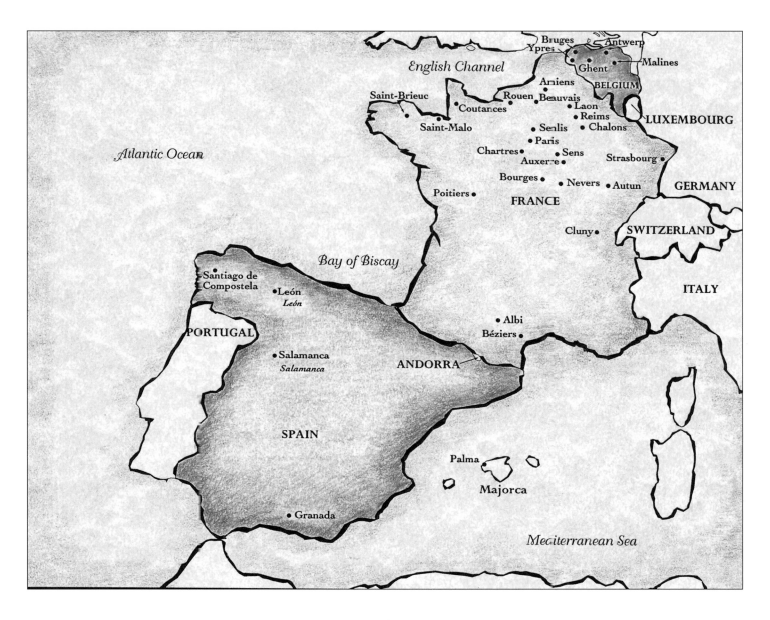

RIGHT: Exterior of the east end of the Cathedral of Saint-Cécile, Albi (Tarn), France. Begun in 1282, in the aftermath of the Albigensian Crusade, and consecrated in 1480, Albi has been called "a fortress against heresy." Note the narrow windows, which look like arrow slits, as compared to the usual Gothic expanses of glass.

OPPOSITE, TOP: The Cathedral of St. Rombaut, Malines (Mechelen), Belgium, was begun in 1212 but was largely rebuilt after a fire in 1341. The massive west tower, begun in 1452, was planned to be 550 feet (167.6m) tall, but the plan was modified in the sixteenth century and the tower is only 320 feet (97.5m) in height. The tower was damaged by shelling during the First World War, but has been restored.

OPPOSITE, BOTTOM: Begun in 1352 and completed in 1584, the Cathedral of Onze Lieve Vrou, Antwerp, Belgium, was originally designed to have two west towers. The 400-foot (121.9m) north tower was not completed until the sixteenth century; the south tower was left unfinished. Like a number of other Belgian churches, Antwerp's design is derived in part from that of Belgian town halls. Note how the cathedral stands in the midst of the city, unlike the typical English cathedral with its surrounding green.

OPPOSITE, TOP: Upper part of the north portal of the Cathedral of Santa María de Regla, León, Spain. The Gothic cathedral of León succeeded a Romanesque cathedral that was destroyed at the end of the twelfth century. The cornerstone for the new building was laid in 1199, but construction did not begin until around 1255. The cathedral, which was modeled on French cathedrals and followed the floor plan of Reims, was consecrated in 1303.

OPPOSITE BOTTOM: The Cathedral, Palma de Mallorca, Spain, 1230–1513. In 1229 King James I of Aragon conquered the island of Majorca from the Moors. In 1230 the cathedral was begun at Palma, the island's capital, but most of the building was done during the fourteenth century. The cathedral is one of Spain's largest, and its 144-foot (43.9m) nave vault is unusually high.

LEFT: The New Cathedral at Salamanca, Spain, was begun in 1513 but was not completed until the eighteenth century. The New Cathedral was one of the last Gothic cathedrals built in Spain. When it was constructed, the Old Cathedral (begun in the twelfth century) was left standing, so Salamanca has two connected cathedrals. The 361-foot (110m) sixteenth-century tower was encased in masonry in the mid-eighteenth century, after it had been weakened by an earthquake.

ABOVE: This detail of the New Cathedral's west portal (circa 1530) is a fine example of late Gothic sculptural decoration.

CHAPTER FIVE

CATHEDRALS OF GERMANY, AUSTRIA, THE CZECH REPUBLIC, AND SCANDINAVIA

The frontier of the Roman Empire ran along the Rhine, so only a very small part of modern Germany was within the Roman Empire. The Franks, who conquered Gaul in the fifth and sixth centuries, also expanded eastward, defeating the Alemanni and converting them to Christianity. Under Pepin the Short and Charlemagne, Christian missionaries were sent to proselytize the pagan Saxons and Bavarians, and both peoples were subsequently conquered by the Franks. These conquests can be said to have begun the *Drang Nach Osten* ("push to the east")—an expansion of German territory that lasted until the fifteenth century and extended as far as Estonia. This expansion was carried out by German nobles and (from the thirteenth century on) by the Order of the Teutonic Knights, and was at the expense of Slavic and Wendish peoples, many of whom were pagans.

Germany was the first of the Frankish territories to recover from the ninth-century breakdown of central authority brought about by territorial division and Viking and Magyar (Hungarian) raids. By the early tenth century, the wild Magyar horsemen were raiding different parts of Germany on an almost yearly basis. In 919 the German nobles decided that they needed a strong ruler to defeat the Magyars, and they elected as king Henry the Fowler of Saxony (reigned 919–936), the most powerful of the German dukes. Henry and his son Otto I "the Great" (r. 936–972) defeated the Magyars and restored order in Germany, and in 962 Otto went to Rome and had himself crowned emperor, thus reviving what was later to be called the Holy Roman Empire. In the process Otto asserted German control over northern Italy.

The Ottonian emperors used bishops in their administrations and gave their bishops substantial rights and powers. One by-product of the bishops' new administrative importance was the building of a number of monumental new cathedrals. These Romanesque structures continued the Carolingian tradition of the westwork but often increased the number of towers. The cathedral at Worms, for example, had a west tower over the entry, two flanking west towers, a tower over the crossing, and two east towers. Elements from northern Italy, such as raised choirs built above crypts, were also introduced. Until the late twelfth century, most German cathedrals were built with flat roofs.

Between 1076 and 1122 the German emperors were involved in the Investiture Controversy, a struggle with the papacy for control over the Church. The Investiture Controversy was accompanied by widespread local warfare in Germany and the rise of feudalism. During the twelfth and thirteenth centuries, Germany was divided by dynastic struggles between the Welf and Hohenstaufen families. The Hohenstaufen usually (but not always) were the imperial party; the Welfs led the nobles, and were generally supported by the pope. The result of this century and a half of intermittent conflict was the inability of the German emperors to establish a centralized royal authority. Late in the twelfth century, Henry VI of Germany (r. 1190–1197) married the heiress of the Norman Kingdom of Sicily and South Italy. Their son Frederick II (r. 1197–1250) made Italy his main base of power. To secure Germany, he made major concessions of rights and privileges to the German nobility. When Frederick II's son Conrad IV (r. 1250–1254) died, the German monarchy became elective and German kings lost many of their remaining powers. Germany became a collection of virtually independent principalities, cities, and territories, and continued as such into the nineteenth century. Some cities joined the League of Rhenish Towns or the Hanseatic League—the latter to become a great confederation of northern European commercial towns. Both leagues were based on the principle that if the German kings could no longer adequately protect the towns, the towns would unite and protect themselves. As

PAGES 76–77: View of Cologne Cathedral, Rheinland-Pfalz, Germany, from the River Rhine. Begun in 1248 and not completed until 1880, Cologne is a cathedral of superlatives. In addition to its great size and the long period required for its completion, it has twin towers that rise some 515 feet (157m) above the ground, making it one of the tallest cathedrals in Europe. Although much of the city of Cologne was destroyed by British bombs during World War II, the cathedral survived despite a number of direct hits.

ABOVE: The exterior of the west apse at Worms Cathedral, Rheinland-Pfalz, Germany, was completed around 1230. The cathedral of Worms was begun in the early eleventh century but was substantially rebuilt in both the early and late twelfth century. The surviving structure is from the late twelfth and the thirteenth centuries. Like the other great Rhenish Romanesque cathedrals (Mainz, Speyer, and Trier), Worms has apses at both the east and the west ends.

OPPOSITE: View of Limburg an der Lahn Cathedral, Hessen, Germany, from the east. Begun in 1213 and completed in 1242, Limburg's transitional Gothic cathedral was built on the site of a tenth-century church. The seven-towered structure is situated in a picturesque location on a rock above the River Lahn. The cathedral's decoration was restored in the 1970s.

in tenth- and eleventh-century France, some bishops were lords of their towns. Other towns were largely independent. As was true elsewhere, financial prosperity and civic rivalry were manifested in the building of cathedrals.

Gothic architecture came to Germany from France in the mid-thirteenth century. Among the transitional German cathedrals were Freiburg im Breisgau, begun around 1170 in the Romanesque style but with a middle of the thirteenth-century Gothic nave; Limburg an der Lahn, consecrated in 1235; and Naumburg, enlarged after 1250. The first fully German Gothic cathedral was begun at Cologne in 1248 on a plan that made it the largest Gothic cathedral in northern Europe. This cathedral was an expression of the prosperity of Cologne, whose archbishop was one of the electors of the German king. While early German Gothic cathedrals generally had twin west towers, like French cathedrals, a later development was the single west tower, as at Freiburg and Ulm. Another popular German Gothic form was the so-called hall-church whose nave and aisles were the same height—this design was applied to cathedrals (as at St. Stephen's in Vienna) as well as to churches.

Perhaps because the income of German cities depended on trade, a number of German cathedrals took an unusually long time to complete. This was particularly true of cathedrals built on very large plans, such as those at Cologne, Ulm, and Regensburg. All three cathedrals were finally completed in the nineteenth century, during the period in which Germany was unified and became a major European power for the first time since the Middle Ages.

Austria was originally the German East March (Ostmark), and was the southeastern frontier of Germany; it remained within Germany and the German Confederation until 1866. The historical background for the cathedral architecture of Austria is for the most part similar to that of Germany.

While German architecture had an important influence on Czech and Scandinavian cathedrals, other national architectural traditions were

ABOVE: In the mid-thirteenth century, the cathedral at Naumburg, Saxony, Germany, was enlarged by the addition of a second choir at the west end of the building. In this choir, built in the Gothic style, were placed life-size statues of the eleventh-century founders of the cathedral—eight men and four women. Shown here are Margrave Ekkehard of Meissen and his wife Uta—two outstanding examples of early Gothic German sculpture. These statues date from the third quarter of the thirteenth century.

also significant. The Czech Republic is composed of Bohemia and Moravia, both of which were part of the ninth-century Great Moravian Empire. This area lay between Germany and the Byzantine Empire, and missionaries from both the Latin West and the Greek Orthodox East attempted to convert the Slavic population. In the last third of the ninth century, the famous Orthodox missionaries Cyril and Methodius established Christian communities in Moravia, but papal opposition and the destruction of the Moravian Empire by the Magyars in the early tenth century largely eliminated Orthodox influence. Bohemia was converted during the tenth century, and there German influence led to the adoption of Latin Christianity, which ultimately became the religion of Moravia as well. Moravia was incorporated into Bohemia in the early eleventh century.

From the tenth to the beginning of the fourteenth century, Bohemia was ruled by the native Premyslid dynasty. However, as Germany expanded, Germans began to settle in Bohemia and establish towns; in time the towns became largely Germanized, while the countryside remained Slavic. The thirteenth century was a period of substantial prosperity, and the king of Bohemia became one of the electors of the German Empire. In 1306 the last Premyslid king was assassinated, and after several years of political conflict the Bohemians elected John of Luxemburg (r. 1310–1346) as their king. John's son Charles (r. 1346–1378) was crowned emperor in 1355, and under the French-speaking Luxemburg dynasty Bohemia became one of Europe's leading cultural centers. Gothic painting flourished, and in Prague a university was established and St. Vitus' cathedral was begun, though it was not completed for almost six hundred years.

Christianity came indirectly to Scandinavia. Early English and Carolingian missions were not successful, but during the ninth century many Viking raiders and Viking conquerors of other parts of Europe converted to Christianity, and some of them returned home and brought their new religion with them. By the tenth century there were Christian communities in various areas of Denmark, Norway, Sweden, and Iceland. In Norway the spread of Christianity was associated with centralization or expansion of royal authority and was accompanied by a good deal of violence. Both Olaf Tryggvason (r. circa 996–1000) and St. Olaf Haraldsson (r. 1015–1028) were Christians, and the miracles attributed to St. Olaf after his death provided Norway with a royal martyr and Scandinavian Christianity with a central focus. Conversion in Denmark and Sweden also accompanied royal centralization, but was accomplished more peacefully than in Norway. King Harald Bluetooth of Denmark (r. 936–986) was baptized around 968 and fostered Christianity, but not until his grandson Canute's reign (1018–1035) were permanent Danish sees created. While the conversion of Sweden is credited to King Olaf Skötkonung (r. 1000–1024), it was not in fact completed until almost a century later. German missionaries played a more important role in Sweden than elsewhere. In Iceland the decision to convert was made by the national assembly (Althing) after a peaceful debate in the year 1000. The conversion of Finland came by way of Sweden in the mid-twelfth century, and one of the key figures in the establishment of a Finnish Christian church was the Englishman Henry of Uppsala. Finland was part of Sweden until 1809, when it was annexed by Russia. One result of this conquest was a growth in the influence of the Russian Orthodox Church.

Because Christianity came to Scandinavia relatively late, Scandinavian cathedral architecture was strongly affected by foreign influences. Nidaros Cathedral in Trondheim was influenced by English models, Roskilde resembles northern French cathedrals in a number of respects, while the towers of Lund Cathedral show a German influence. Another trend—also a result of the period when building began—was that a num-

ber of Scandinavian cathedrals were begun in the Romanesque style but completed in Gothic. The development of the Orthodox Church in Finland that resulted from the annexation of Finland by Russia early in the nineteenth century led to construction of Finnish Orthodox churches and an Orthodox cathedral in the Russian style.

ABOVE: The top of the tower and steeple at Ulm Cathedral, Baden-Württemberg, Germany. After withstanding an imperial siege in 1376, the citizens of the free city of Ulm decided to build a new hall-church befitting Ulm's wealth and prestige. The ambitious west tower was begun in 1392, but building proceeded intermittently. During a building campaign in the late fifteenth century cracks appeared in the tower, and in 1529 the project was abandoned. The tower and steeple were finally completed in 1890. At 528 feet (160.9m), Ulm's tower is the tallest stone church tower in the world.

LEFT: The west front of Freiburg im Breisgau Cathedral, Baden-Württemberg, Germany, circa 1200–1513. The Romanesque church of Freiburg was remodeled in the Gothic style in the mid-thirteenth century. The single west tower was completed in the mid-fourteenth century. Its 377-foot (114.9m) openwork spire became a model for other German spires, both at the time and during the nineteenth century, when the builders of Cologne's west spires and Ulm's spire used Freiburg as a model.

BELOW: Exterior of the Gothic choir, 1355–1413, at Aachen Cathedral, Nordrhein-Westfalen, Germany. Aachen was the coronation church of the German emperors, and was also a pilgrimage church that housed a notable collection of relics, including the shrine of Charlemagne, who had been canonized in 1165 by an antipope. In 1349 the emperor Charles IV was crowned at Aachen, and not long afterward he had work begun for the cathedral's new Gothic choir, which was modeled on the Sainte-Chapelle, the French court chapel in Paris.

OPPOSITE, TOP: The west towers of the Frauenkirche, Munich, Bavaria, Germany, 1468–1525. Munich's brick Gothic cathedral was built on the site of an earlier Romanesque church and was largely completed in twenty years. In 1525 the 325-foot (99.1m) towers were capped by the copper onion domes that have become the symbol of the city. The Frauenkirche became a cathedral in 1469. In April 1945, after successive Russian and German bombardments, the cathedral caught fire and much of it was destroyed. It has since been restored.

OPPOSITE, BOTTOM: The roof and the south tower of St. Stephen's Cathedral, Vienna, Austria, 1304–1510. In 1304 the Hapsburg emperor Rudolf IV had Vienna's parish church raised in status to an independent collegiate church. At the same time, a new Gothic choir was begun as a hall-church extension of the existing Romanesque structure. Originally two transept towers were planned, but only the 450-foot (137.2m) south tower (1368–1433) was completed.

LEFT: Aerial view of Salzburg Cathedral, Austria, 1614–1655. Salzburg was ruled by its prince-archbishops until it was secularized in 1802. Its Romanesque cathedral burned down in 1598 and was replaced by the present early Baroque structure based on Italian models. Note the octagonal central dome.

ABOVE: Interior of the central dome at Salzburg. The paintings depict the Evangelists and scenes from the Old Testament. The dome collapsed as the result of an air raid in 1944; the paintings were restored when the dome was rebuilt after the Second World War.

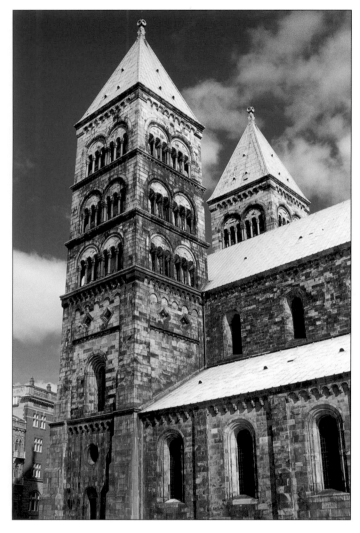

LEFT, TOP: The western towers of Lund Cathedral, Sweden. The cathedral of Lund (then in Denmark) was begun around 1080 and expanded after 1103, when Lund became the seat of the first Scandinavian archbishop. The high altar was consecrated in 1146, and the western towers were begun soon after. The cathedral was damaged before the Reformation by several fires and suffered neglect after the Reformation; it has subsequently been restored several times, most recently in the nineteenth century.

LEFT, BOTTOM: View from the choir of Roskilde Cathedral, Denmark, looking east. Begun around 1170, the present cathedral is the fourth church on the site. The east end was started in Romanesque style but was revised in the Gothic style before the choir was completed. The building was essentially finished by 1275, the western towers were completed around 1400, and the spires were added in 1635–1636. Note the contrast between the Romanesque rounded arches of the east end and the Gothic pointed arches of the choir.

RIGHT: View of St. Vitus' Cathedral, Prague, Czech Republic, from the southwest. When Prague was raised to an archbishopric in 1344, King John of Bohemia began the building of a new Gothic cathedral to replace the existing Romanesque work. The first architect chosen was a Frenchman who had worked at Avignon. On his death in 1352, Charles IV chose Peter Parler, a young architect who had worked at Cologne. Parler, his sons, and his brother became the premier Gothic architects in Europe, and under them the first stage of the building of St. Vitus was completed (1353–1420). Later stages begun during the sixteenth, seventeenth, and eighteenth centuries were interrupted for various reasons, and the cathedral was not completed until 1929. The great south transept tower, shown on the right, was begun by Parler (1396–1406) and given a Renaissance gallery in 1560–1562; its steeple was added in 1770.

CHAPTER SIX

CATHEDRALS OF ITALY

Christianity came early to Italy. Saints Peter and Paul were both martyred in Rome during Nero's persecution of the Christians (64–66), and by the end of the second century the Church in Rome may have been the largest single Christian community. Urbanism was also well developed in Italy, and it has been estimated that by the mid-third century, at a time when Christianity was still illegal, Italy had around one hundred bishops. In all, some 350 Italian towns are or have been the sites of cathedrals.

The third century was a time of economic and population decline throughout the Roman Empire, and towns were particularly hard hit. After Christianity was legalized, not every town was able to build a large cathedral, though churches were built everywhere. Many of the smaller towns supported only one congregation, so their bishops continued to serve primarily as priests rather than as the administrator-bishops that were characteristic of larger cities.

The emperor Justinian's reconquest of Italy in the sixth century brought the Byzantines into the area, though the Lombards conquered much of the peninsula in the late sixth and seventh centuries. Byzantine forces remained in Italy until the eleventh century, and Byzantine architecture continued to be an important influence on Italian cathedrals, particularly in Sicily, southern Italy, and Venice.

PAGES 88-89: Detail of facade and bell tower, the Duomo, Florence, Tuscany, Italy. The exterior of the Duomo is finished in white, green, and red marble. On the right is Giotto's 292-foot (89m) bell tower.

ABOVE: View of the cathedral of Pisa, Tuscany, Italy (1063–1272), from the southwest. The cathedral of Pisa was begun in 1063, a year after the Pisan fleet had won a major naval victory against the Moslems off Palermo. The exterior of the cathedral is built of white marble, and the four-story arcade of the facade was widely imitated in central Italy. At the right is the freestanding bell tower (1174–1350) familiarly known as the Leaning Tower of Pisa.

During the eighth century, the popes called in the Franks to defend the papacy against the Lombards. Both Pepin the Short and Charlemagne invaded Italy and defeated the Lombards, and Charlemagne's coronation as emperor at St. Peter's in 800 set a precedent: the emperors were thereafter to be crowned by the popes at Rome. In the tenth century the German kings, starting with Otto I, claimed the imperial title and sovereignty over northern Italy. However, the emperors could only exert effective control over the area when they were actually present, and during most of the High Middle Ages Italian nobles and, later, Italian city-states dominated northern Italy.

Northern Italy was one of the earliest areas in western Europe to see the revival of cities and the growth of long-distance trade and commerce. This revival was under way by the year 1000. Venice and Genoa became major seaports, while other Italian cities such as Florence and Milan developed thriving industries in woolen goods and metalwork, respectively. With their new wealth the cities established militias and were able to assert their authority over the surrounding countryside. Some nobles moved into the new city-states voluntarily; others were defeated and forced to live within town walls. The result of these developments was a great increase in both prosperity and civic pride—qualities which manifested themselves, as elsewhere, in the building of cathedrals.

In central Italy, however, the popes were able to expand their territorial authority and even to develop a state of their own. When Pepin the Short defeated the Lombards, he gave the papacy a substantial grant of land in central Italy—the Donation of Pepin of 756. However, not until the eleventh century was the papacy able to free itself entirely from control by local nobles and the German emperors so that the popes could act effectively as territorial rulers.

ABOVE: Aerial view of the cathedral of Cefalu, Sicily, Italy (1131 to mid-thirteenth century), looking northeast. Cefalu was begun by King Roger of Sicily in 1131, a year after his coronation. Like other Norman Sicilian cathedrals, Cefalu contains Byzantine, Moslem, and Norman motifs. Compare the decorative interlaced arches just below the roof on the north transept and north side of the choir with the round Romanesque arches on the exterior of the cathedral of Pisa.

careers as mercenaries and ended as great territorial lords. Tancred's son Count Roger I of Sicily (reigned 1072–1101) reconquered Sicily from the Moslems, and Roger's son Roger II was crowned king of Sicily in 1130 and reigned until 1154. Local church building reflected the influences of the peoples and traditions that characterized particular regions.

The so-called First Romanesque style began in northern Italy around the year 800. The style was based on the architecture of Ravenna modified by forms derived from surviving ancient Roman buildings. The Italian Romanesque period lasted through the twelfth century. Building styles varied considerably from region to region, but in general Italian Romanesque cathedrals followed the basilican plan, many cathedral facades were characterized by ornamental arcades, separate bell towers were

Southern Italy was characterized by a variety of different peoples and traditions. During the ninth century, Sicily was conquered by Moslems from North Africa who remained on the island for more than two centuries. On the mainland there were both Lombard and Byzantine territories, and in the early eleventh century a new element was added when Norman adventurers came to southern Italy to seek their fortunes. Among the Normans were the sons of Tancred of Hauteville; they began their

often constructed, and colored marbles and mosaics were used more frequently in decoration than in other parts of western Europe.

Toward the end of the twelfth century, the Gothic style was brought to Italy and used in the construction of churches built by Cistercian monks. Although it was adopted by both Franciscan and Dominican friars, this new architectural style did not affect Italian cathedrals until fairly late in the thirteenth century, and its greatest impact then was felt in northern and central Italy. By that time the Western emperors were no longer an effective force in Italian politics, and the cities of northern Italy and the papacy had become fully independent. Italian prosperity continued throughout the thirteenth and the first half of the fourteenth century in spite of frequent warfare—first against the last Hohenstaufen emperors, Frederick II (r. 1197–1250) and his son Conrad IV (r. 1250–1254), and later among various cities as well as between factions within cities. However, Italy's central location in the Mediterranean, her thriving industries, and her lead in new banking techniques more than made up for the losses of war.

The great prosperity of the mid-thirteenth century led directly to the building of imposing new cathedrals at Siena and Florence. In Milan, a century later, cathedral building resulted from a combination of prosperity and the personal ambition of Duke Gian Galleazo Visconti. At Orvieto the impetus for building the cathedral was a miracle: while celebrating mass in Bolsena (a small town near Orvieto) in 1263, a visiting priest who had been troubled by doubts about the actuality of the transubstantiation of bread and wine saw drops of blood emerge from the eucharistic wafer and stain the corporal cloth. Pope Urban IV was in Orvieto at the time, and he commanded that the cloth be brought to that city, where it was enshrined in a magnificent reliquary. In the following year Pope Urban inaugurated the annual Feast of Corpus Christi to celebrate the institution and gift of the Eucharist and the miracle of transubstantiation. Overnight, Orvieto became a pilgrimage center, and in 1290 a new cathedral was begun.

Italian Gothic differs in a number of respects from Gothic elsewhere. Italian Gothic cathedrals have much less stained glass than Gothic cathedrals elsewhere: while there are large rose windows, the other windows tend to be relatively small. The roofs of Italian Gothic cathedrals are low-pitched or flat, and large domes are an important external feature. Decoration of facades is provided by mosaics as well as by sculpture, and the use of contrasting building materials (as at Orvieto and Siena) is particularly striking.

Early in the fifteenth century, Italian architects developed the Renaissance style, which is characterized by the introduction into new buildings of Roman architectural elements. The result was a simpler, more classical architecture without the many spires that often characterized Gothic churches. Classical columns (Doric, Ionic, Corinthian, and Tuscan) were reintroduced, and buildings were designed on a more symmetrical plan than was the case with Gothic structures. A number of Italian churches in the Renaissance style were built at this time. St. Peter's at Rome is the one great Italian Renaissance basilica, though elements of Renaissance design are found in cathedrals begun in other styles—for example, the dome of Florence's cathedral.

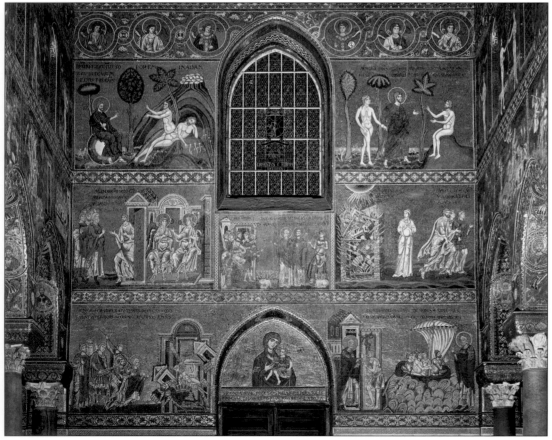

OPPOSITE, TOP: The west front of Monreale Cathedral (1174–1182), near Palermo, Sicily. Monreale cathedral was built by order of King Roger's grandson William II (r. 1154–1189). The west front with its two square towers (the left one incomplete) and its eighteenth-century portico hardly suggests the wonders to be found inside the cathedral.

OPPOSITE, BOTTOM: The nave of Monreale has many splendid Byzantine mosaics dating from the last quarter of the twelfth century, including cycles of scenes from the Old and New Testaments. The details shown here depict the creation of Eve at the upper left, Lot's wife as a pillar of salt at the middle right, and the Byzantine Virgin and Child in the arch above the door.

LEFT: The late-twelfth-century cloister of Monreale Cathedral. Monreale was a monastic cathedral, but of the adjoining monastery only the splendid cloister survives. Each of the cloister's more than two hundred paired capitals is different.

ABOVE: Detail of columns in the cloister of Monreale Cathedral, also from the late twelfth century. The marble columns shown here contain glass mosaic inserts.

LEFT, TOP: Detail of the thirteenth-century mosaic in the vault of the Chapel of Cardinal Zen at St. Mark's Cathedral, Venice, Italy. Venice was in constant contact with Byzantium throughout the Middle Ages, and Venetian art and architecture were strongly affected by Byzantine influences. In the eleventh century the body of the apostle Mark was brought to Venice, and in 1063 the church of San Marco was begun above the tomb. In this mosaic the saint is shown asleep in a boat in the Venetian lagoon. An angel appears to Mark in a dream and tells him that someday his body will be received here with great honor.

LEFT, BOTTOM: The thirteenth-century facade of Amalfi Cathedral, Campania, Italy. Amalfi was an important seaport until 1137, when the town's forces were defeated by those of Pisa. Amalfi's early medieval cathedral has been remodeled many times. It has mid-eleventh-century Byzantine bronze doors and a bell tower (left) dating from 1276 with a glazed-tile roof exhibiting Moslem influences. The cathedral was redecorated in the Baroque style in the eighteenth century, and the facade was rebuilt after it collapsed in 1861.

OPPOSITE: The upper part of the facade of Orvieto Cathedral, Umbria, Italy (1290 to sixteenth century). Orvieto's facade is very much like a triptych, with wings on each side of the central panel. The facade was designed by the Sienese architect Lorenzo Maitaini around 1310 but was not completed until the late sixteenth century. The mosaics were restored during the seventeenth and eighteenth centuries.

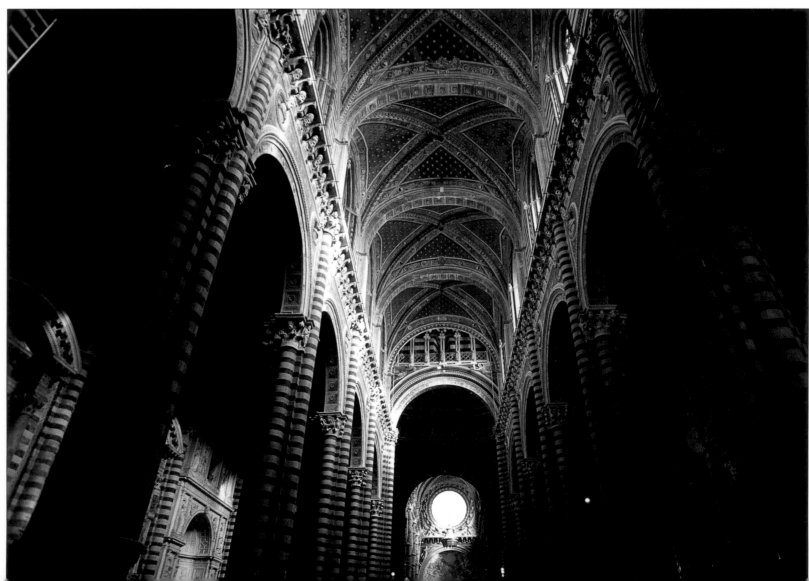

OPPOSITE, TOP: View of the cathedral of Siena, Tuscany, Italy (1179–c. 1380), from the west. The cathedral of Siena was begun in the Romanesque style but was largely rebuilt in the Gothic style starting in the second half of the thirteenth century, when construction was supervised by Cistercian monks. The dome was finished in 1294, the bell tower in 1313; the upper facade, modeled on that of Orvieto, was not finished until the second half of the fourteenth century. In 1339 an enormous new nave was begun, but work was interrupted by the Black Death and was never resumed.

OPPOSITE, BOTTOM: View of the interior of Siena Cathedral, looking west. The alternating bands of black and white marble on the walls and columns create a dramatic impression. Note the round arches of the choir and the pointed arches of the vault.

ABOVE: The Duomo, Florence, Tuscany, Italy. In 1294 the citizens of Florence decided to replace their small early-Christian cathedral; construction was completed in 1462. The new Gothic cathedral was built on a giant scale—it is 490 feet (149.4m) long and about 350 (106.7m) feet high—and for a time the Duomo was the largest cathedral in Italy. Its architects have included some of the greatest figures in Renaissance art: Arnolfo di Cambio (1245?–1302); Giotto (1267?–1336), who planned and began the bell tower to the left of the cathedral; and Filippo Brunelleschi (1377–1446), who built the dome that was the model for the dome of St. Peter's in Rome.

OPPOSITE: Distant view of St. Peter's Basilica, Rome, Italy (1506–1626). The domes of St. Peter's in Rome and St. Paul's in London are perhaps the best-known church domes in the world. Unlike London, Rome has preserved much of its Renaissance skyline, so the modern visitor can still get the same sense of power, majesty, and scale that the inhabitants of Rome felt when St. Peter's dome was completed some four hundred years ago.

RIGHT, TOP: Interior of the apse of St. Peter's Basilica. At the right is the chair of St. Peter, sculpted by Bernini from 1656 to 1666, which encloses the chair that traditionally belonged to the saint. Above the chair, in the center of the round window, is an image of the dove of the Holy Spirit. Soaring above all is the interior of Michelangelo's mighty dome (1547–1593), which has been called "the greatest creation of the Renaissance."

RIGHT, BOTTOM: The west front of the cathedral of Milan, Lombardy, Italy. Milan's Gothic cathedral was begun in 1386 but was not completed until the nineteenth century. Its building was greatly encouraged by Milan's first duke, Gian Galeazzo Visconti (r. 1395–1402). Many of the architects who helped design the cathedral were French or German, including a member of the Parler family, so the cathedral is not in the mainstream of Italian architectural development. Next to Seville, Milan is the largest Gothic cathedral in the world, which helps explain why it took so long to finish. The facade was completed by Napoleon between 1805 and 1809. Note the neoclassical pediments above a number of the lower window arches.

CATHEDRALS OUTSIDE WESTERN EUROPE

From its inception, Christianity sought to bring its message to places outside its area of origin. Christianity may have reached Persia as early as the first century and was introduced into Ethiopia during the fourth century. According to tradition, St. Thomas was the apostle to India, and India certainly had Christian communities before the end of the fifth century. However, the expansion of Islam from the seventh century on sharply curtailed Christian growth in all these areas.

In eastern Europe, Byzantine missionaries successfully converted many of the Slavic peoples during the ninth century, and in the 860s the Bulgarian king Boris I (r. 852–889) accepted Greek Orthodox Christianity. The widespread introduction of Christianity to Russia also resulted from a royal conversion—that of Grand Prince Vladimir of Kiev (r. 980–1015) around the year 987. After the fall of the Byzantine Empire to the Ottoman Turks in 1453, Russia became the center of Greek Orthodox Christianity. Over the centuries the Russians developed their own style of cathedral architecture, based in part on the Byzantine cruciform pattern and in part on local traditions, though outside influences also played a significant role. Ivan III "the Great" (r. 1462–1505) brought

103

Italian architects to Moscow, and the Cathedral of the Dormition of the Virgin in the Kremlin (built between 1475 and 1479) was designed by the Bolognese architect Aristotle Fioraventi. With its cruciform plan, central dome, and four corner domes, this building became a model for many subsequent Russian cathedrals. Another motif, the tent-style roof, can be seen in St. Basil's Cathedral (1555–1561), also in Moscow.

From the thirteenth to the fifteenth century, Franciscan and Dominican missionaries were sent to North Africa and the rest of the Moslem world, to northeastern Europe, and as far east as Mongol China. The main success of these missionaries was in eastern Europe, where they assisted in the conversion of the Prussians and the Lithuanians. Christian communities were established in China, but these probably did not survive to the end of the fifteenth century.

Large-scale growth of Christianity outside western Europe began in the fifteenth century and was part of the general expansion of Europeans into new geographical areas. During the fifteenth and sixteenth centuries, Portuguese missionaries were at work along the coasts of Africa, in the

Congo Valley, in India and the East Indies, in Japan, and in Brazil. The Spanish brought Catholicism to the Americas and to the Philippines. Much of the Portuguese and Spanish evangelization was done by religious orders: by Franciscans, Dominicans, and Augustinians, and by the Jesuit order founded in the 1530s. The missions met with varying degrees of success. In the Americas and the Philippines, the Roman Catholic Church flourished. In Africa, India, and China, it met with relatively little long-term success, and in Japan it was systematically wiped out in the seventeenth century.

During the same period, Protestant missionaries also engaged in evangelical work, but since not all Protestant sects have bishops, their settlements were not always characterized by the building of cathedrals. In North America, cathedrals were built first by the Spanish and the French, and not until much later by English-speaking colonists. With the expansion of the British Empire in the eighteenth and nineteenth centuries, Anglican cathedrals were built in areas as far apart as Australia, Canada, and Africa. The great nineteenth-century immigration to the United States from Roman Catholic countries such as Ireland, Italy, and Catholic Germany led to the building of cathedrals in the larger cities.

As one would expect, cathedral architecture in colonial areas was often based on architectural models from the mother country. The sixteenth-century Spanish cathedrals in the New World were built in Spanish Gothic-Mudejar and Renaissance styles. The Anglican cathedrals built throughout the British Empire in the nineteenth and early twentieth centuries were generally in the Gothic Revival style, as were many of the cathedrals built in the United States during the same period. In the twentieth century, cathedral architects have been more concerned with building in accordance with local tradition, as at Nairobi, or in using new building materials to represent important Christian symbols, as in Brasília and in Garden Grove, California.

PAGES 102–103: St. Basil's Cathedral, Moscow, Russia, 1555–1560. The Cathedral of the Intercession, later called St. Basil's Cathedral, was built by Tsar Ivan IV "the Terrible" (r. 1533–1584) to commemorate his victory over the Tatars and the conquest of the city of Kazan in 1552. The cathedral is located in Red Square, just outside the Kremlin. The central tower, with its tentlike roof, is surrounded by eight chapels, each with a differently patterned dome. An elevated gallery encircles the entire structure.

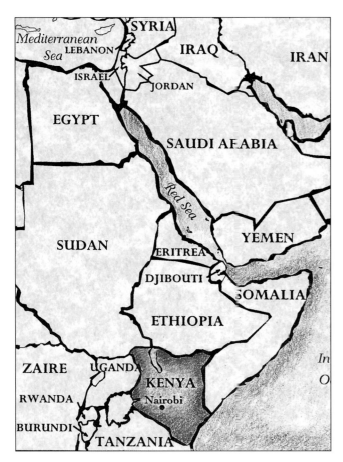

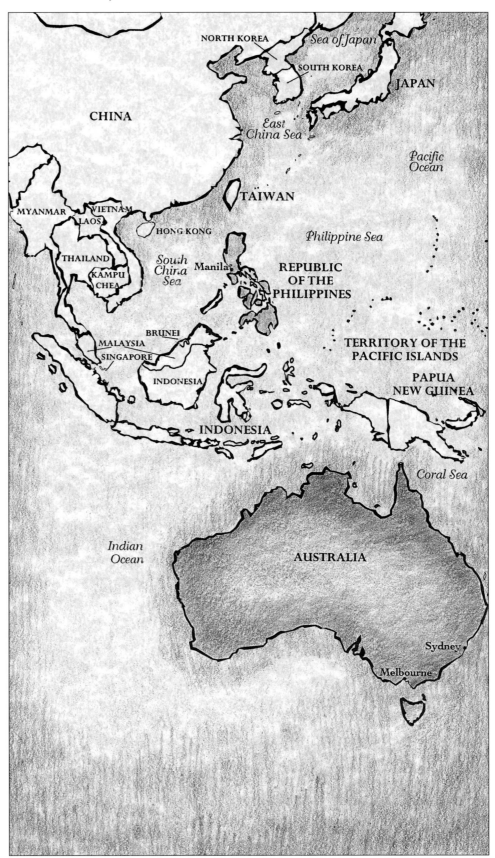

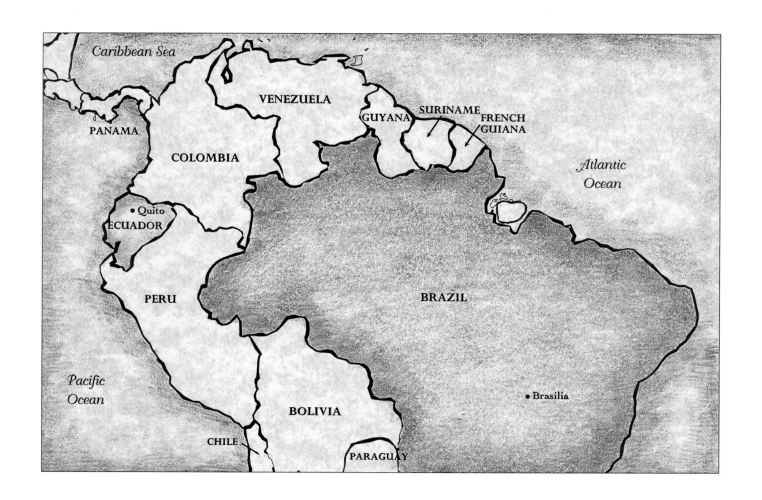

LEFT: Smolensk Cathedral, Russia, 1524–1525. The Russians conquered Smolensk from the Lithuanians in 1514 and soon afterward began building the fortified Novodevichy Convent to defend Moscow from the southwest. The cathedral was built within the monastery walls and was modeled on the Cathedral of the Dormition in Moscow. However, the cathedral of Smolensk is surrounded on three sides by a covered gallery (foreground).

RIGHT: Alexander Nevski Memorial Cathedral, Sofia, Bulgaria, 1882–1912. This cathedral, built to commemorate the Russian liberation of Bulgaria from the Turks in 1887–1878, was named after the patron saint of Tsar Alexander II (r. 1855–1881). Designed by a Russian architect, Sofia Cathedral is the largest cathedral in the Balkans.

OPPOSITE, TOP: The Cathedral of the Holy Family, Nairobi, Kenya, was built between 1960 and 1963. This modern cathedral of concrete, glass, and local stone has been said to "successfully retain the atmosphere of Kenyan culture." The cathedral reflects the position of Roman Catholicism as Kenya's leading religious denomination.

OPPOSITE, BOTTOM: Interior view of Manila Cathedral, Republic of the Philippines, looking east. Built between 1954 and 1958, the present cathedral is the sixth on the site. The first was built of wood in 1581 and was destroyed by fire two years later. Three subsequent cathedrals were destroyed by earthquakes in 1600, 1645, and 1863. The fifth cathedral was destroyed in 1945 during the last stages of the Second World War. Note the lines of chapels flanking the nave.

OPPOSITE: The transept of St. Mary's Roman Catholic Cathedral, Sydney, Australia. St. Mary's is built on the site of Sydney's first Roman Catholic chapel, which was begun in 1829 and burned in 1865. The new cathedral, started in 1868, was built on a monumental scale in Gothic Revival style. The building is 350 feet (106.7m) long and more than 150 feet (45.7m) high. It was consecrated in 1882, but the west towers were not finished until 1929 and the spires planned for the towers were never added.

LEFT, TOP: North view of the cathedral at Quito, Ecuador, from the Plaza Independencia. Built between 1562 and 1565 by Spanish architects in the Gothic-Mudejar style, the cathedral was solemnly consecrated in 1572. Its exterior walls contain memorial plaques to colonial leaders, and inside the cathedral is the tomb of Ecuador's liberator, Antonio Sucre (1793–1830). The cathedral has been reconstructed several times as a result of earthquake damage.

LEFT, BOTTOM: Interior view of the cathedral of Brasília, Brazil, which was completed in 1966. The glass dome over concrete ribs representing Christ's Crown of Thorns allows worshipers to see the sky. This design can be seen as a modern expression of the Gothic emphasis on greater light and space. The dome is 108 feet (32.9m) high and 197 feet (60m) in diameter.

RIGHT: St. James Cathedral, Toronto, Canada. St. James Cathedral is built on the site of Toronto's first church, which was built of wood in 1807 and enlarged in 1818. The church was rebuilt in stone in 1834 but burned down five years later. A new church was built in less than a year and was consecrated as a cathedral by Toronto's first bishop, but this new cathedral survived for only ten years before being destroyed by yet another fire. The present Gothic Revival cathedral was begun in 1850 and completed in 1876. St. James's 318-foot (97m) spire is the tallest church spire in Canada.

ABOVE: View of the choir from the nave of the Episcopal Cathedral of St. John the Divine, New York City, United States. St. John the Divine was begun in 1892 in a neo-Romanesque style, but in 1911 the architects were changed and building continued in a neo-Gothic style based on thirteenth-century French cathedral architecture. Note that the lower part of the choir is Romanesque but the arches are Gothic. The cathedral remains incomplete; when finished it will be the world's largest cathedral.

The west towers of St. Patrick's Roman Catholic Cathedral, New York City, United States. St. Patrick's Cathedral was designed by James Renwick Jr. and modeled in part on Cologne Cathedral. When St. Patrick's was built (1858–1888), its site was on the northern edge of New York City, and the 330-foot (100.6m) towers, completed in 1888, were landmarks for many years. Today St. Patrick's is in the middle of Manhattan and the towers are exceeded in height by a number of surrounding buildings, but the structure remains the largest Roman Catholic cathedral in the United States and one of New York City's most famous buildings.

OPPOSITE: View of the Cathedral Church of St. Peter and St. Paul, Washington, D.C., United States, from the southwest. Built between 1907 and 1990, this Episcopalian cathedral is also known as Washington Cathedral and as the National Cathedral. Built in English Gothic Revival style, the structure dominates the District of Columbia skyline. The cathedral's chapels are used by many religious groups, and in this way the cathedral realizes George Washington's dream of a great national church.

LEFT, TOP: One of Washington Cathedral's neo-Gothic gargoyles.

LEFT, BOTTOM: The Garden Grove Community Church, Garden Grove, California, United States, widely known as the Crystal Cathedral, was built between 1977 and 1990, and is not a cathedral at all. It is, however, an excellent example both of modern trends in cathedral architecture and of the new situations cathedral builders will have to face. The Crystal Cathedral was designed by Philip Johnson and John Burgee for televangelist Dr. Robert Schuller. The "cathedral" proper is star-shaped and constructed of glass over a steel frame. It was designed to bring sunlight to the congregation. The building is fully media-equipped and has 90-foot (27.4m) electronically controlled doors that can be opened to allow people in the parking lot to view the service. The church interior was designed so that more of the congregation is close to the pulpit than in traditional churches. The freestanding spire is made of polished stainless steel.

GL⊕SSARY

ambulatory: An aisle behind the choir or behind an altar; walks in cloisters and galleries can also be called ambulatories.

apse: The semicircular or polygonal end of a church.

arcade: A series of arches supported by columns.

archivolt: A band of carved molding or sculpture on the face of an arch.

atrium: A courtyard, usually enclosed by colonnades, in front of a cathedral.

baptistery: A separate building or part of a church in which the rite of baptism is administered.

basilica: In ancient Rome, an oblong building used as a hall of justice; in the early Christian era, a church built on the plan of such a hall; today, a Roman Catholic church with special liturgical privileges.

buttress: An external support generally built against the outside of a masonry wall.

canon: A member of the clergy of a secular cathedral who receives a share of the cathedral's revenues.

capital: The molded or sculptured top part of a column.

catechumen: In the early Church, a person being taught the doctrines of the Church before receiving baptism— a neophyte.

cathedral chapter: A body of canons responsible for the operations and government of a cathedral.

cathedral precinct: The grounds immediately surrounding a cathedral.

chancel: Originally the space immediately around the altar of a church reserved for the clergy and usually enclosed; also called the "sanctuary" or the "presbytery." Today, the body of the church east of the nave and transepts. See also **choir**.

chantry chapel: A chapel built and endowed for the purpose of saying masses and offering prayers for the souls of the founder and his designees.

chapel: A part of a church with a separate altar, set aside for prayer. See also **chantry chapel** and **Lady chapel**.

chapter house: A separate building or room in which the chapter of a cathedral meets.

choir: Originally a part of a church between the nave and sanctuary where the singers (choir) sat. Today the term is often used interchangeably with "chancel."

clerestory: An upper story of the nave of a cathedral with windows for illumination.

cloisters: A covered walkway with an open arcade surrounding a courtyard.

crossing: The intersection of the nave and transepts in a cruciform church.

dean: The official, ranking just below a bishop, who heads a chapter and supervises cathedral services.

diocese: The territorial district under the authority of a bishop.

flying buttress: An external arch transmitting thrust to a buttress and used to brace the upper walls of a cathedral to help carry the weight of the roof or vault.

gallery: An open upper story above an aisle of the nave.

hall church: A church in which the aisles and the nave are close to the same height.

high altar: The main altar of a church, located at the east end.

Lady chapel: A chapel dedicated to the Virgin Mary.

lantern pillars: Pillars supporting the lantern.

Mudejar: Architecturally, Spanish Christian architecture influenced by Moorish elements.

narthex: A vestibule between the main entrance and the nave of a church.

nave: The part of a church in which the congregation sits or stands.

nave altar: An altar in the nave.

paganism: A polytheistic religion; heathenism.

pier: A solid masonry support.

portal: An imposing entry to a church.

Reformation: The sixteenth-century religious movement that resulted in the founding of Protestant religious groups.

roof boss: An ornamental projection covering the intersection of vaulting ribs in a roof or ceiling.

scissor arch: An interior support resembling an open pair of scissors.

see: Narrowly, the official seat (cathedra) of a bishop. In a broader sense the term can refer to the town in which the bishop has his seat or even to the entire diocese.

spire: A tall, tapering, pointed structure on top of a tower or roof.

strainer arch: An archlike interior buttress used to absorb thrust and keep walls from leaning.

transept: An arm of a cruciform church at right angles to the nave and choir.

tympanum: The space beneath an arch above a doorway, often filled by sculptural relief.

vault: An arched structure often forming a ceiling or roof.

vaulting: An arched construction.

westwork: The tall western front of a Carolingian or Romanesque church, including the tower(s) and portal.

BIBLIOGRAPHY

Brivio, Ernesto. *Repertorio delle cattedrali gotiche*. Milan: Fabbrica del Duomo di Milano, Nuove edizioni Duomo, 1986.

Conant, Kenneth John. *Carolingian and Romanesque Architecture, 800 to 1200*. 4th ed. London: Penguin, 1993.

Davies, Martin. *Romanesque Architecture: A Bibliography*. New York: G.K. Hall, 1993.

Florisoone, Michel. *Dictionnaire des cathédrales de France*. Paris: Larousse, 1971.

Frankl, Paul. *Gothic Architecture*. Harmondsworth, Middlesex: Penguin, 1963.

Harvey, John Hooper. *Cathedrals of Spain*. London: Batsford, 1957.

Histoire générale des églises de France, Belgique, Luxembourg, Suisse. Paris: R. Laffont, 1966–1971.

Kleinbauer, W. Eugene. *Early Christian and Byzantine Architecture: An Annotated Bibliography and Historiography*. Boston: G.K. Hall, 1992.

Krautheimer, Richard. *Early Christian and Byzantine Architecture*. 4th ed. Harmondsworth, Middlesex: Penguin, 1986.

New, Anthony S.B. *A Guide to the Cathedrals of Britain*. London: Constable, 1980.

Pevsner, Nicolas. *The Cathedrals of England*. Harmondsworth, Middlesex: Penguin, 1985.

Teague, Edward H. *Index to Italian Architecture: A Guide to Key Monuments and Reproduction Sources*. New York: Greenwood Press, 1992.

White, John. *Art and Architecture in Italy: 1200 to 1400*. 3rd ed. New Haven, Conn.: Yale University Press, 1993.

INDEX

PH⊕T⊕GRAPHY CREDI†S